Y2K FAMILY SURVIVAL GUIDE

**Jerry MacGregor
and Kirk Charles**

HARVEST HOUSE PUBLISHERS
Eugene, Oregon 97402

THE Y2K FAMILY SURVIVAL GUIDE

Copyright © 1999 by Jerry MacGregor and Kirk Charles
Published by Harvest House Publishers
Eugene, Oregon 97402

Library of Congress Cataloging-in-Publication Data

MacGregor, Jerry.
    Y2K family survival guide / Jerry MacGregor and Kirk Charles.
        p.   cm.
    ISBN 0-7369-0164-7
    1. Survival skills.   2. Year 2000 date conversion (Computer systems)
I. Charles, Kirk.   II. Title.
GF86.M33   1999
363.34'97—dc21   98-55223
                                                                        CIP

Printed in the United States of America.

99 00 01 02 03 / BC / 10 9 8 7 6 5 4 3 2

For Patti and Susan

CONTENTS

PART ONE

THE BIG PICTURE

ONE

What's the Big Deal?

I magine you're at a party celebrating the new millennium when suddenly the lights go off. Your appliances won't work, you have no heat, and you can't call anyone to complain because your phones are on the blink. The next day you awake to find you have no water, you have to walk to the store because your new car won't start, but the stores are empty anyway because they did not receive any deliveries. There are no radio or television transmissions being received, even on your battery-powered receivers, so you have no idea what is happening around the rest of the world. You start to worry about your safety, since there are no working alarms, and you're not even sure you could get hold of the police or fire department in an emergency. The next day you discover your office computers are down, you can't communicate with clients or customers, so everyone is asked to "stay home and keep calm."

What's Ahead

- **The Reality of Y2K**
- **What Is Y2K?**
- **Certain Uncertainty**
- **A Double-Digit Dilemma**
- **Mainframe Madness**
- **Why Didn't Programmers Anticipate the Problem?**
- **How Does Y2K Affect Me?**
- **The Three Scenarios**

That's when you discover the downtown area is being patrolled by National Guard units.

The news finally starts to filter in from various sources. Asia has gone black—there is no power at all, putting a stop to nearly all import and export business. A number of terrible air crashes occurred when jumbo jets ceased functioning properly, or simply could not find their way safely to the ground due to massive power outages at landing sites. Criminal gangs are battling police for control of the inner cities, leading to the government declaring martial law. There are even reports of riots in suburban neighborhoods, as people begin to panic over scarce food, drinking water, and firewood. The stock market goes into collapse, and you begin to wonder if your position at work is safe, or if your business can even survive. If only you had planned better, perhaps you'd have been more prepared. You get ready for bed that night in a cold house, with a loaded gun on top of your dresser....

Or maybe you dreamed it all. There are a few days of intermittent power problems, and some unprepared countries suffer, but by and large the promised computer glitches turn out to be nothing more than a mere inconvenience. Within a few weeks government and business have solved the most important crises, and you're back to your old lifestyle.

Both of these scenarios are possible. In fact, there are experts on each side declaring them as fact. The issue driving the potential problem is called Y2K—an acronym for the "year 2000."

The Reality of Y2K

Y2K is the computer-driven crisis that threatens to hamstring the world's computers on January 1, 2000. Some are predicting it will bring the end of the world as we know it. Others foresee only a brief, inconvenient snag in the fabric of life, on a par with a serious winter storm, but no major catastrophe. Often their widely divergent opinions are drawn from the same information. Between these two polarized viewpoints, another possibility is that the disruption will be more than a hiccup but less than full cardiac arrest. Anyone who has studied the underlying issues would agree that some level of disruption is inevitable, but despite all assurances, nobody really knows how bad it's going to be. Those who are prepared will certainly be able to weather the storm—however strong the winds—more easily than those who refuse to plan ahead.

Claims and assurances by those who say the problem will not be severe should be evaluated in light of the overall size and complexity of the situation. Unlike a winter storm which strikes a limited area or region, *Y2K will hit everywhere in the world on the same day*. Rather than one part of the country responding in compassion, as happened after Hurricane Andrew decimated Florida a few years ago, no section of the country will be unaffected. People in the north will be just as hard-hit as those in the south, and it's possible that access to needed resources won't be immediately available. The truth is nobody knows how severe and long-lasting the effects of Y2K will be, but wisdom would say, "Develop a survival plan, just in case."

We know the precise moment when the brunt of the storm will hit, even if we don't know how hard she'll blow. In the time that remains before Y2K, it would seem only prudent for a family to take precautions and prepare for the uncertain days ahead. This book was written to help you reflect on the problem, develop a reasonable plan to ready yourself, and help your friends and neighbors be equipped for either a mild or moderate disruption of American life. The Bible tells us to trust in God, but we can also be prepared for emergencies.

What Is Y2K?

When you hear people discuss Y2K, your response probably falls into one of four camps:

1. *You may be uninformed.* That is, you may know that Y2K has something to do with computers and the turn of the century, but you have no idea how it will affect your life, if at all. To those of us who have been monitoring the situation for some

time and have begun to prepare simple survival plans, it is amazing how many people still have no idea what Y2K is. The more people who remain in the dark, the greater the potential for disaster from even a moderate interruption of basic services.

2. *You may be in denial.* You might dismiss the warnings of disaster as merely the ranting of doomsayers trying to sell books and newsletters. Maybe you've looked into Y2K and can't believe everything could be so far out of control, or maybe you're confused by all the uncertainty. Denial may lead you to think, "Until I can see it clearly, I'm not going to call it a problem. I'll cross that bridge when I get to it." But if you wait until the problems are obvious (and many would say they already are), it will be too late. Instead, embrace the uncertainty. Accept the reality that we just don't know how bad it's going to be, and make the most prudent plans you can with the information you have available. For example, if this were a coming blizzard, would you want to store food and blankets? Those who grew up in snow country recognize it is better to be overprepared than to be underprepared.

3. *You may be paralyzed.* One thing Y2K has in abundance is uncertainty. Not knowing what to do can lead to paralysis. Think of it this way: If you are climbing a mountain and don't know which way to jump, it's often easier to stay put, especially if all the available options require risk or sacrifice. Unfortunately, if you stay in one place, you'll die of exposure. You may be tempted to panic, but even panic requires action you aren't prepared to take. So if your inclination is to say, "Y2K is too overwhelming; I don't want to think about it," consider this: Which is more overwhelming, taking prudent precautions today, or suffering unprepared in the days to come?

4. *You may be prepared for Y2K*—or at least you've decided to begin preparations. Maybe you haven't started because you don't know what to do. Regardless of where you are right now, this book will show you practical ways to begin to develop a survival plan for yourself and your family. Our aim is not to predict how big the problem will be, although as you will quickly see the ramifications are global, interconnected, and complex.

There have already been many books published, articles written, and web sites established to inundate you with information from credible sources about the scope and nature of the Y2K dilemma. But while several authors have risen to the task of identifying the problem, we haven't seen many that have laid out a systematic solution for how the average family—one that doesn't have a mountain retreat or a hidden farm in the country—can protect itself against the possibility of worldwide social upheaval.

Our goal is to give uninformed readers enough information to prompt them to action, and enough resources to help them devise a prudent plan for survival. For those in denial, we hope to convince them the problem is big enough to require a solution. For those who are paralyzed, our practical suggestions will help get them moving on a plan of action. And for those who are already planning or who are ready to begin preparation, we offer a comprehensive guide that considers three possible scenarios: a two- or three-day disruption, a monthlong disruption, or a yearlong disruption.

The amount of information available about Y2K is staggering, and it would be easy to get bogged down in a lengthy discussion of the problem. However, other writers have taken up that calling. We want to move you beyond the stage of speculation about how mild or monstrous it might be, and get you to implement an action plan to prepare your family as best you can for whatever unfolds at the start of the year 2000.

Certain Uncertainty

The one constant in every Y2K scenario is uncertainty. Our advice is to use that uncertainty as a catalyst for action. Uncertainty can prompt us to carefully study a situation and become better-informed, then devise a plan that moves us in a reasonable direction toward safety. We believe everyone should take three important steps: *Become informed* about Y2K (it isn't going to vanish into thin air), *decide* how you will respond, and *take appropriate action* in a way that makes the best use of your available resources and present circumstances.

Even among supposedly computer-savvy individuals, the awareness of Y2K has dawned slowly. Starting with a complete lack of awareness, someone hears about the problem for the first time, but thinks, "It doesn't affect me. I've got a Mac."

When they realize Y2K goes well beyond desktop computing and will touch everyone in the world, the next logical thought is, "Surely someone will find a cure." When they come to understand there is no magic solution, they begin to see the scope of the problem but feel helpless to do anything about it. Denial or paralysis may set in. The next step is to realize that something must be done, for the problem cannot be ignored. Once someone decides to become informed and develop a survival plan, resources such as this book can be used to put into action a sensible, well-organized strategy that balances one's present circumstances with the available options and opportunities.

A Double-Digit Dilemma

How did we get into this mess? In the early days of large-scale computing—back when data entry was a punch-card process, disk space was at a premium, and computer memory was an expensive commodity—programmers routinely conserved space by recording dates using only *two digits for the year.* Accordingly, the year 1959 would be represented simply as 59, 1972 would be 72, and so on. Consequently, when the year 2000 arrives, right on schedule and hard on the heels of 1999, those two-digit codes will come up 00, which many mainframe computers and embedded chips will interpret as the year 1900 instead of 2000. Suddenly, every date-sensitive formula that hasn't been corrected will be recalculated using 1900 as the base year. (On some PCs, the default year may be 1980 or 1984, depending on the year the operating system was developed.)

When this happens, the computers will either freeze up or shut down, producing erroneous data based on faulty date-code calculations, or creating other errors which may go undetected until much later. Because these computers are networked with other computers worldwide, and since many businesses and government agencies exchange information electronically as a part of daily commerce, this double-digit dilemma could become a global disaster overnight. Even Y2K-compliant computers may be affected by faulty information passed along the network by other noncompliant computers. Any calculation that is age- or date-sensitive could be affected.

Why can't the experts write a software program that searches for errant date codes and makes the necessary corrections? While simple in concept, the problem with Y2K stems from the compounded complexity of most computer systems and software programs, plus the widespread distribution of billions of embedded microchips, many of which may be noncompliant but which cannot be easily accessed or fixed.

Programmers back in the 1960s and 1970s assumed the applications they were designing would be obsolete long before the turn of the century, so the two-digit date code didn't seem to be a problem. In fact, it was a sign of good, efficient programming not to include extra characters. If the old programs had run their course and been replaced by newer, Y2K-compatible systems, or if four-digit date codes had become standard when the cost of memory and storage became affordable, we would not be staring down the barrel of Y2K with the overwhelming prospect of widespread computer failures on January 1, 2000. The two-digit date-code problem was perpetuated for decades, affecting countless systems and applications. We simply do not have enough time to fix every computer before the hard-and-fast Y2K deadline.

Mainframe Madness

Although the physical size of computers has shrunk as we've found ways to pack more power onto tiny microchips, and desktop computers are now common, *mainframe computers* are still essential workhorses for government agencies, public utilities, telecommunications companies, banks and other financial institutions, transportation companies, and many other businesses. Many mainframe computers are running proprietary software programs that were designed for specific applications within the organization. Some of these custom packages have been modified, upgraded, and patched together over the years by a variety of programmers, often without adequate documentation of the changes. Before long, the simple little problem of two-digit date codes was endlessly multiplied and widely distributed. Many of these systems have been quietly running in the background for decades while the programmers who designed them have long since retired, died, or moved on to other companies.

Today, *many organizations have tens or hundreds of millions of lines of code that must be corrected to avoid Y2K problems*. Some of these programs are written in programming languages that are no longer widely used, which means qualified personnel may not be available to correct the problems. Even where qualified programmers are available, there are not enough of them to tackle all the code that must be modified—and certainly not before the end of 1999. The software industry has always valued shortcuts and streamlining, but these very same shortcuts disrupt the correction process. The lack of precise documentation of changes hampers the ability of programmers coming in to fix programs they didn't design and have never worked with.

Fixing the problem is a tedious, time-consuming process of identifying where the faulty date codes are, checking and fixing millions of lines of computer code, and then testing the fixes to make sure they are Y2K compliant—all the while hoping the "fix" doesn't cause other problems or introduce bugs into the system. Next, the individual system must be brought back online and tested to make sure the fixes are compatible with other computer systems. Already we've seen companies that have experienced problems during the fix-and-test process. One problem with a single satellite knocked 90 percent of the world's pagers off the air in 1998 during a Y2K compliance test. In 1997, an entire ATM network was shut down by the failure of a single networking device. These examples suggest that at least some level of disruption is inevitable, even in isolated systems. The daunting prospect of Y2K is that, because of global networking and commerce, *no system is truly isolated.* Widespread, simultaneous failures of systems could set off a domino effect around the world.

The magnitude and scope of the Y2K problem is difficult to explain without sounding like an alarmist. But even the rosiest of optimists would say, "Don't take Y2K lightly." Even if enough time were left to fix every computer, the estimated cost of all the repairs would range between 200 billion dollars to upwards of 850 billion dollars. To make matters worse, not only do we have millions of "legacy systems" still in operation, but newer applications were often written using bits of code from the older programs, thereby incorporating defective date-sensitive code into these new programs and systems.

Further, because users historically have not wanted to scrap older applications in favor of new, the newer programs and applications were forced to be "backwards compatible," which means cutting-edge applications may still incorporate noncompliant date codes in order to maintain compatibility with older versions and applications.

Why Didn't Programmers Anticipate the Problem?

If the Y2K problem was identified years ago, why wasn't something done sooner? The best way to answer that question is to *look at your own response to Y2K.* If you are only now beginning to think seriously about the problem, you're already late to the dance and your window of opportunity for planning and preparation is rapidly closing. Programmers and other computer professionals were slow to respond to the dangers of Y2K back when prompt action could have headed off the coming crisis. For companies with hundreds of interrelated systems and hundreds of millions of lines of code to correct, the time to start responding was at least two or three years ago—long before Y2K began to make headlines. As a society, we have learned to place a lot of faith in the computer industry to come up with bigger, better, less-expensive solutions, and we have been lulled into complacency by the naive notion that someone somewhere would find a cure for this problem.

Information systems departments were slow to respond to the emerging crisis in the early and mid 1990s. Procrastination and complacency played a large role. Many were hoping and waiting for a "silver bullet" solution to be developed that would solve the entire predicament quickly and easily. Even when it became apparent no magic cure would solve the complex Y2K issues, many programmers (or their corporate decision-makers) still did not assign the necessary resources to address the situation. Many companies were unwilling to invest the large sums of money and time necessary to fix the problem until it became obvious that ignoring Y2K was a worse option.

In addition to denial and foot-dragging, competing priorities got in the way of a timely and adequate solution to Y2K. The world did not stand still to wait for programmers to catch up. Until recently, many companies tried to solve the Y2K problem on the fly, fixing lines of code as they came up in daily use. Only lately have many organizations begun to dedicate significant resources to the issue of Y2K compliance. Even today, political, financial, legal, and other concerns still cloud the picture for many corporations. However, you should know that *the federal government, your local government, and every large corporation is taking the Y2K threat seriously.*

Visit any U.S. government web site and you'll find a discussion of Y2K problems. Talk to your local utility company and you'll discover they are already making plans for power outages. Inner-city police departments have talked openly about working with National Guard troops to patrol the streets in the early days of the year 2000. It's a real problem, and it isn't going to disappear.

How Does Y2K Affect Me?

In our opinion, Y2K is a threat to everyone because of the widespread, pervasive use of computers. Think about all the ways you depend on computers today. Even if you don't use a PC at home to balance your checkbook, even if you have somehow remained computer illiterate all these years, *you depend on computers in almost every area of life.*

All record keeping, billing, paying, tax collection, government services, and most accounting programs are stored on and controlled by computers. All bank transfers, stock transactions, and other investments are managed by computers, including your 401k, corporate pension plan, and individual investment portfolio. Railways, still a vital link in the energy-production and food-distribution systems, depend on computerized switches to coordinate trains.

Computers are used to route air transportation, including passenger reservations and baggage handling. Air traffic control systems and radar systems utilize embedded microchips to monitor and control vital functions. December 31, 1999, will probably be a good day to find lots of empty parking spaces at your local airport. Even some of the more optimistic Y2K prognosticators are saying the airline industry is one of the most vulnerable sectors of the economy, and many would say that airborne over the Atlantic is the last place they would want to be when the clocks turn over to the year 2000.

Computers monitor power transmissions between local and regional utilities to optimize equipment usage and avoid system overloads. Power companies share electrical power with each other across regional power grids. A blackout in one part of this system could have an adverse effect on the delivery of electricity hundreds or thousands of miles away. If the power goes out for a significant amount of time, our plugged-in society screeches to a halt.

Computers handle the complex switching requirements for telephones and other telecommunications equipment, routing calls, calculating charges, and balancing loads across the network. Many businesses rely heavily on the phone system for voice, data, and fax transmissions.

The government uses mainframe computers for all of its important functions, including receiving and disbursing checks.

The IRS uses mainframe computers to collect the tax revenues that fund all of the government's programs, including Social Security, welfare, Medicare, and Medicaid. Each of these programs and hundreds of others use computerized systems that are at risk. Most reports indicate that the Social Security Administration, welfare, and Medicare/Medicaid systems have made more progress toward Y2K than other government agencies, but none of these systems is yet 100 percent compliant. Millions of people nationwide depend on regular, timely checks from these agencies, and any disruption or delay in the process would be felt immediately and dramatically.

Military weapons and missile-guidance systems are controlled by computers, as are satellite tracking and surveillance equipment. Weapons systems that the United States has sold to other countries around the world are also at risk, as well as weapons manufactured by other nations. The possibility of regional or global military destabilization as a result of Y2K cannot be ignored.

In addition to all the vital functions controlled by programmable mainframe computers and PCs, billions of embedded microchips, many of which are nonprogrammable and date-sensitive, monitor factory emissions and safety systems, burglar and fire alarm systems, backup lighting systems, security cameras, air traffic control systems, radar systems, traffic lights, global positioning system receivers, oil and gas pipelines, photocopiers, video cameras, voice-mail systems, cellular telephones, laptop computers, automobile fuel mixtures and engine heating and cooling, telephone switches, medical equipment, ATMs, credit-card systems, and countless other processes and systems. A malfunction in an embedded controller can shut down an entire system, even if no other problem exists.

Computers process large amounts of information quickly, perform calculations based on numerical formulas, and pass information along to other computers in the form of coded transmissions. Think about all the possible disruptions to your daily life if even a fraction of these computers went out because of Y2K. Then consider the ramifications if the failures are wide-spread.

When drafting the chapters for this book, we grappled with the question of what tone to adopt. It is difficult to delve beneath the surface of the Y2K story without becoming shocked and risk being dismissed as alarmists. Several individuals have been ringing the warning bells for the past few years, but they have often been ignored or criticized. We also recognize that ultimately, our lives are in the hands of God more than in our own planning and devices. Yet we don't think planning is at odds with faith. It is reasonable for a Christian to take steps to protect the future, at the same time recognizing the Lord's control over events. With that in mind, your best approach would be to evaluate the evidence for yourself, then make an informed decision about how much preparation you think will be necessary for your family.

The Three Scenarios

Part of the uncertainty surrounding Y2K has to do with how long the difficulties will last. Obviously, a power outage that lasts a month is a bigger problem than a blackout that lasts two or three days. *Our approach is to suggest plans for the short-term (The Two-to Three-Day Plan), the mid-term (the One-Month Plan), and the long-term (the One-Year Plan or more).* If the problems persist for a year or more, the result will be a drastic change in life as we know it, and the magnitude of such an occurrence would likely overwhelm even the best-laid plans. Even if our preparations come up short, at the very least we will have bought ourselves some time to adapt to the emerging new realities.

The three scenarios we have identified differ from each other by a factor of ten. A month is ten times longer than three days, and a year is roughly ten times longer than a month. If the problems last for a few days, your primary concerns will be heat, light, water, food, and medical necessities. If the crisis lasts for a few weeks or a month, the above concerns will be magnified, and your job and housing may also be threatened. You will have to consider your need for cash, how to handle waste (both garbage and bathroom waste), and your family's personal security. Civil unrest may become a factor as those who failed to prepare begin to suffer and look for ways to alleviate their suffering.

If the crisis lasts for a year or more, every need listed above will increase tenfold, and your very survival may be in jeopardy. Unless you have planned well, your housing, employment, and access to food and water will be affected. Civil unrest will most certainly become a factor long before the one-year mark. Our longer-term planning takes into consideration the possible escalation of conflict brought about by lingering disruptions or failures in key sectors of society.

So reflect on Y2K for a minute . . . do you think it is a short-term problem? If so, look carefully at our suggestions for a two- or three-day emergency plan. Do you think it will be a more significant problem? Then you need to begin planning, using our one-month recommendations. Do you think Y2K will be a long-term problem? In that case, consider the suggestions we make for the one-year plan. The choices you make now will prepare your family for survival in the future.

T W O

Why Should I Care?

- On January 1, 2000, some people will still be uninformed—they won't know what hit them.
- On January 1, 2000, some people will still be in denial—they won't admit they've been hit, or recognize what's going on.
- On January 1, 2000, some people will still be paralyzed—and they'll be so overwhelmed they won't be able to move quickly enough to save even what they have left.
- On January 1, 2000, some people will be panicking—and they will be the most dangerous of all.
- On January 1, 2000, the people who planned ahead and prepared for the unknown will have their best-laid plans tested and found either adequate or insufficient. They will suddenly be everyone else's best friend.

Today is the day to decide: *Which group will you choose to join?* After you've finished this book you'll no longer be uninformed, so take your pick from the other four groups. As for us and our families, we're going to be as prepared as we can be. Denial and paralysis are not effective strategies for coping with Y2K. Unless you've taken precautions and put a

---

What's Ahead

- **Learning from the Past**

- **Isolated Problems or Widespread Disaster?**

- **Hope for the Best, Prepare for the Worst**

plan in place, panic will be your only other option. Don't procrastinate. Time is of the essence. Uncertainty and the need to make decisions without full information is part of the challenge of responding to the Y2K problem.

Learning from the Past

The seers who are predicting the end of the world as we know it *sound* extreme, leaving us to wonder, "Could it really be that bad?" But once you have examined the evidence for yourself, you may be asking, "How can it *not* be as bad as they say?" It may be hard for many people in the United States to imagine drastic changes in our style and standard of living, but we would do well to look back 70 years at a couple of life-changing, globally impacting events that occurred earlier this century and realize that worst-case scenarios are not necessarily farfetched.

Put yourself in the place of a German Jew in the late 1920s. Life might not have been perfect, but the overall cultural climate was not bad. Within a decade, however, normal life had taken a drastic, irreparable turn. Most Jews never saw it coming. Even when the Gestapo began to arrest some and destroy their places of business, others stayed put and hoped it wouldn't happen to them. When the war started and rumors began to circulate about death camps, many throughout Europe and the United States were in denial, not willing to believe things could really be that bad. Until the first of the concentration camps was liberated five years later, the full horror of what had happened was largely unknown.

Does the enormity of the Holocaust mean that Y2K will be as bad? Of course not—we're simply drawing a comparison to the radical, life-altering impact a tumultuous and unanticipated change can have on society. In some respects it might be easier to imagine a ruthless dictator rising up and killing millions of innocent people than it is to fathom an otherwise innocuous computer-programming decision turning the industrialized world on its ear. Y2K is not a sinister conspiracy to alter the course of history, nor a plot hatched in a smoky back room.

Instead, it is an unforeseen but nonetheless powerful glitch in our computerized, information-driven world.

In the late 1920s, boundless optimism and booming markets were brought to a crashing halt, sparked in part by a profound loss of consumer confidence. The Great Depression changed not only our perspective of wealth, but our American lifestyle. The current bull market on Wall Street presents an eerie foreground to the imminent arrival of Y2K. The parallel is not just that the stock market could crash again, but that the lingering aftershocks of a significant social upheaval could be felt for more than a few days, weeks, or months. The Great Depression lasted close to a decade and brought about significant changes in the relationship between the government and the governed. Come January 1, 2000, *something is going to happen that will affect our lives—possibly for a long time*. How drastic the change will be and how long-lasting the results remains to be seen, but the fundamental question that everyone should be asking is, "Am I prepared?"

The intent and scope of this book is to recognize that not everyone has the resources or the inclination to "run for the hills" (and running away to hide may not be the most prudent strategy anyway), but everyone can do something to prepare for the effects of Y2K.

Perhaps the most compelling reason for immediate action is the practical reality of supply and demand. As more people become aware of the problem and the steps necessary to prepare, the demand for certain items such as generators, toilet paper, ready-to-eat meals, camp stoves, wood stoves, propane, water purification devices, storage containers, nonperishable foods, and portable toilets is certain to rise—and prices are bound to rise as well.

A parable is told in the Bible about ten young ladies who took their lamps and went to wait for the bridegroom's arrival. Five brought along extra oil, in case the groom was delayed, but the other five had only the oil in their lamps. While they were waiting, all ten of the maidens fell asleep. When the shout went up that the bridegroom was arriving, the young ladies awoke and trimmed their lamps. Only those five who had brought extra oil had enough to relight their lamps and greet the groom. The others were forced to go last-minute shopping—at night—not a very promising prospect for success.

In the parable, the timing of the bridegroom's arrival was uncertain, and all of those waiting fell asleep. With Y2K we know exactly when the main impact will hit, and we cannot afford to be lulled to sleep. Those who have the foresight to bring some extra "oil" will be ready to respond to the challenge. Everyone else will be forced to fend for themselves as best they can, unless the prudent ones set aside enough "oil" to share as well. Wouldn't you rather be on the side of the prudent and the prepared?

Some preparation is better than no preparation, and the better your plan, the better your chances of coming through intact. If you don't make provision for yourself and your family, you not only put yourself at risk, but you also become a burden to those who have prepared, or you endanger the entire community when you are forced by necessity to survive without available resources.

Keep in mind that Y2K will strike not only across North America in the midst of winter, but around the world. We've come to expect the government to bail us out of catastrophes through disaster-relief programs and special appropriations, but if the government itself is affected by Y2K, who's going to step in with relief? Even if the power company restores service, it may take a few days before they get to your neighborhood. Even if federal disaster relief is available, it may take weeks to reach your area. If you have prepared even minimally, you increase your chances of surviving until longer-term solutions can be implemented.

Isolated Problems or Widespread Disaster?

Most of the arguments suggesting that Y2K will be a tempest in a teapot and cause only limited and localized disruption are centered on the premise that the vast majority of mission-critical functions will be Y2K-compliant before January 1, and any other problems will be minor enough to allow for repairs within three days, or a week at the most. If those projections are correct, only a bit of individual preparation is necessary. Most people will ride out the storm unscathed. The problem with this not-to-worry scenario is that it hinges entirely on the ability of governments and businesses around the world to limit the scope of their computer-related problems in a world of interrelated and interdependent systems. The potential for a widespread impact is exacerbated by seven effects, any one of which could cause disruption on its own, but which in concert escalate the potential for disaster dramatically. It is these seven effects that lead us to believe more than a perfunctory level of preparation is required to protect yourself and your family.

1. The Network Effect — For the past few years, companies and government agencies around the world have been working to solve their internal Y2K problems. As 1999 continues, organizations will begin to trumpet their level of Y2K compliance and downplay the importance of where they are falling short. By January 1, 2000, a significant number of organizations will have corrected and tested their mission-critical systems and declared themselves Y2K compliant. The bad news is that *even 100 percent compliance can be sabotaged by the network effect,* which occurs when data from my noncompliant computer infects your clean system because the two are interconnected.

Take the banking industry as an example. Your bank might be 100 percent Y2K compliant, but if a noncompliant bank sends corrupted wire transfers to your bank, the whole system can be affected. Banks are interconnected electronically for the transfer of funds to cover checks, credit-card charges, and automatic deposits and payments. These transactions originate from a wide variety of sources, including credit-card companies, wire-transfer services, banks, and other financial institutions. If one bank has a noncompliant system, it can be locked out of the network to preserve the integrity of the other banks, but only at the risk of undermining the entire system. If a check you try to deposit is drawn on a noncompliant bank, you will likely be denied access to the funds. And if a check you have written must go to a locked-out bank, your transaction could be compromised by its inability to collect the funds behind your check.

The network effect impacts more than just the banking industry. Any business that routinely exchanges information with other businesses is at risk of having bad data transmitted across its networks. The only protection is to avoid any transactions with noncompliant sources (which in itself could cause a major disruption) or to try to filter transactions to detect erroneous data before it hits your system—a hit-and-miss proposition at best.

2. The Spillover Effect — The spillover effect occurs when a failure in one area transfers a load to another area and "overloads" the backup system. *The potential for a problem in one area or system to spill over into another area is part of what makes Y2K so dangerous.*

Telecommunications companies share common switches and sell airtime to each other. When a high volume of calls fills a particular line, the overload of calls can be transferred to another line. But if the overload of calls coming in combines with an already loaded line, the entire system can be tied up in no time. Some advisers recommend you carry a cellular phone in case the land-based lines are all out of service. The spillover effect would suggest that if everyone suddenly switched over to cellular, the increased load on that system would threaten to knock it out as well.

The citizens of Auckland, New Zealand, experienced the spillover effect during a power failure in February 1998, when one of four main power cables servicing the city failed, for reasons never made clear. The sudden loss of the one line transferred the power load to the remaining three cables and knocked them out of service as well. The result was a major city—population 900,000—without power. That meant no lights, no air-conditioning in mid-summer, no elevators in multi-story buildings, and no pumping of water to flush toilets.

Businesses throughout the city were disrupted for weeks. When two of the lines were repaired and ready to be used again, the testing knocked both lines back out of service for several more weeks!

Thousands of power companies across America sell electric power to each other via three interconnected networks that make up the North American power grid. Because many local utilities do not produce enough of their own power to meet peak demands, they buy excess power from other areas to supplement their own production. A short circuit on an Idaho power line in 1996 spilled over onto the network, cutting power to 15 western states and parts of Mexico and Canada. Not only was the loss of power a problem—the attempts at resuming power created headaches as partial power in the lines kept triggering shutdowns of the system. It doesn't take much imagination to see Y2K creating a similar scenario on a nationwide basis.

3. *The Consumer Confidence Effect* — The perception that a problem exists can sometimes create a problem in itself. For example, the global banking system is a powder keg that lacks only a match to set it off. A panic in the financial world could initiate a Y2K crisis long before January 1, 2000. In recent months, we've seen central banks in Russia, Southeast Asia, and Japan come under increased pressure as the global currency crisis has taken root. The effects of Y2K will only increase the pressure on the global financial markets.

When people begin to understand the scope of the Y2K danger, they may respond to their uncertainty with panic, trying to secure hard assets such as cash, precious metals, food, and gasoline. We need only to recall the lines of cars at gas stations during the "energy crisis" of the 1970s to see how quickly a lack of consumer confidence can escalate.

When people begin to respond to their uncertainty about the solvency of the banking and credit industries by trying to liquidate their savings in cash, they will run up against a fundamental weakness in the banking system called "fractional reserves." Because banks make money by lending money, not by holding your deposits and paying you interest, they don't hang on to cash deposits for very long. In fact, when you deposit a check into your account, the only "money" that moves within the system is a credit-and-debit exchange within the Federal Reserve system (tracked and monitored by a mainframe computer). The bank is required to have only enough cash on hand to conduct daily business—which amounts to a small fraction of its total deposits. The cash on hand is available to disburse to the limited number of depositors who ask for it on a daily basis. If everyone were to try to cash out their savings account on the same day, or even try to take out an otherwise modest amount like 2000 dollars, there would not be enough cash on hand at the bank to fulfill the need.

Worse, there is nowhere near enough cash in existence anywhere in the world to supply the need if everyone tried to liquidate their accounts. If everyone in the United States tried to convert two months' salary into cash, the amount of hard currency in existence would be insufficient. The danger of a run on the banks could be the biggest single threat within the Y2K scenario because of the importance of stable currency exchanges in the world economy and the interdependence of every link in the global financial chain. The mainframe connection and global interconnectivity of financial institutions puts every bank at risk.

Global stock markets are also at the mercy of consumer confidence. As long as people trust the long-term prospects of the system and keep a steady hand on their investments, the stock markets may continue to function without much disruption (unless, of course, a system failure corrupts the computer controls). But if a roaring bear takes over the stock market and begins to drive prices down, the stampede could be on, and the spillover to other financial markets could be devastating.

The same principle applies to food and gasoline. Your local grocery store has about three days' worth of food on its shelves. As long as people shop only when they need to, the stores have time to restock and their suppliers have time to keep the pipeline full. But if everyone tries to shop on the same day with the intent of "stocking up," the shelves will soon be picked clean of everything but horseradish. We've seen this phenomenon in limited scope when water, batteries, and candles disappeared from shelves prior to a winter storm.

The consumer confidence effect might also be called the "panic effect," and panic may be the biggest threat to the global system in a Y2K scenario. The possibility for panic seems to rise and fall with the numbers of people in denial about Y2K. If everyone were to gradually implement a prudent action plan, the individual components of the global network might be tested, and some restrictions might need to be imposed to preserve order, but at least the system would have a chance to adapt over time. However, if those in denial suddenly wake up and switch into panic mode, the results could be catastrophic. That's why we are recommending a reasonable and practical action plan that works within the constraints of available resources. Some preparation by everyone is better than full preparation by a few. . . and no preparation by everyone else. That scenario is a recipe for panic and disaster. "Consumer confidence" may be the lighted match that ignites the powder keg of panic, or lights the lantern of reason.

4. *The Domino Effect*—Anyone studying the impact of Y2K quickly recognizes the interrelated dependence of one system on another. Probably the three most vital links in our society are power, communications, and financial transactions. If your home or business is dependent upon power to operate and the power goes out for a significant length of time you may be out of business. *If my business is depending on your business for parts or sales, I may go down with you.* Anyone depending on you would be the next to collapse, and so on. This is called "the domino effect." I can create all the products I want, but if I can't sell them to you or process payments through my bank, I cannot collect the money that is owed to me, and my business will soon fail.

This scenario is merely a microcosm of what might occur simultaneously around the world. The world economy has truly become global over the past several years. Farmers in Iowa depend on grain markets in Russia. Auto manufacturers in the United States depend on parts factories in Asia. Because of the intense interdependence that characterizes the global marketplace, a problem in one part of the world has immediate ramifications around the globe. So even though companies and government agencies in the United States lead the world in Y2K preparedness, a noncompliant foreign trade partner could undermine the entire system.

Computer systems are interrelated, so one bad link has the potential to take down an entire network. Even if 85 out of every 100 stores is Y2K compliant, the noncompliant 15 can undermine the entire system by sending garbled or erroneous inputs to the others. Not only that, noncompliant partners in other countries can negatively affect those in the United States. Even if our systems are 100 percent ready (and no one can be absolutely certain), if any other link in the network is not compliant, our system is at risk.

5. The JIT Effect—A popular business practice in recent years, particularly in the manufacturing sector, has been toward just-in-time (JIT) deliveries of parts and supplies. The reason your local grocery store has enough cartons of eggs to meet the demand, without having tons of spoiled, unsold eggs to throw away at the end of the week, is because of JIT—a method of predicting demand and arranging for supply. The wisdom of such an approach is that less capital is tied up in inventory, and extra supplies on hand are kept to a minimum. One of the results of JIT has been more frequent but smaller orders and shipments, which has helped to revolutionize the freight and delivery industry. But JIT also places a lot of faith on the purchaser's ability to order smart, and the supplier's ability to deliver "just-in-time."

In a climate of disrupted communication and transportation services, JIT all but guarantees a manufacturer will not have adequate inventory on hand to continue to operate very long without fresh supply. We saw the impact of JIT on General Motors recently, when a strike at a single parts supplier shut down 26 GM plants within a short period of time. Imagine businesses and grocery stores unable to predict demand or provide supply. If Y2K seriously interrupts transportation or communication, the effect on business could be immense.

Many individuals manage their personal finances on a JIT basis, living paycheck to paycheck, making payments just in time, and charging the rest to credit cards. The widespread use of JIT adds up to increased vulnerability if the underpinnings of the system—primarily transportation and communication—are compromised.

6. *The Essential/Nonessential Effect* — Many companies have simply waited too long before focusing adequate attention on solving the Y2K problem. With hundreds of millions of lines of code to be repaired and tested before January 1, 2000, businesses have been forced to focus their corrective efforts on "mission-critical" systems—those computers or programs that are the most vital to the survival of the company. The bad news is that *a "noncritical" system in one company may adversely affect a mission-critical system somewhere else.*

Not all interdependencies are of equal magnitude. My business might need you more than you need me. A system you designate as "nonessential" for your company may be critical to me and my business. There has been almost no discussion of the essential/nonessential effect in the Y2K debate.

7. *The Cumulative Effect* — If only one or two of these effects happen simultaneously in a local area, the impact would be noticeable yet perhaps manageable. *But if all of these hit a wide area at the same time, the outcome could be catastrophic.* The essence of the Y2K problem is that many systems over a wide area will be hit, all on the same day. The cumulative effect of these disruptions may total more than the sum of the parts.

Several of these effects are self-compounding as well. Uncertainty breeds more uncertainty. A spillover in one area can start a domino effect in another area, thus creating a new set of spillovers. It is the uncertainty of the cumulative effects that renders meaningless any hopeful assurances that everything is going to be OK, or that the government will be able to step in and solve all the immediate problems. Everything may prove to work, but we cannot know that in advance because it is impossible to accurately predict how these seven effects (and possibly others we haven't thought of) will interplay on or before January 1, 2000. The bottom line: We simply don't know how everything will play out with Y2K.

Hope for the Best, Prepare for the Worst

Although it is widely acknowledged that no "silver bullet" solution will be found to solve the problem, many people still seem to be placing a great deal of confidence in "American ingenuity" to at least mitigate the seriousness of the problem—in fact, we have great belief in America's willingness to sacrifice and serve in order to solve the problem. But it is important to realize Y2K is not a problem only in the United States. It is global, and any country that does business with the United States (which includes everybody who transacts currency on the world market) can have an impact on life here in America. The days of an isolated United States are long gone. Today we live in a global community with a global economy. The results of a problem in one part of the world can have widespread repercussions around the globe. And when you understand that Y2K will hit everyone around the world within 24 hours on January 1, 2000, you can begin to appreciate the enormous magnitude of the problem.

Not everyone is as dependent upon computers and modern amenities as we are in the Western world. The countries and cultures we think of as Third World or "backward" nations will feel much less of an impact. We have more to lose . . . and farther to fall.

The biggest obstacle to global compliance is the lack of time. *It is already too late to correct all the code, test the repairs, and bring every system worldwide into Y2K compliance, but it is not too late to prepare for the inevitable fallout.* You cannot fix all the computers and make the problem go away, but by planning ahead you can take appropriate steps to protect yourself and your family from being overwhelmed. The remaining chapters of this book will help you to get organized and develop contingency plans for your family's survival in the year 2000. The time for action is now.

THREE

When Do I Start?

A city in ancient Israel posted a watchman on the walls, and each sentry understood his responsibility: If he saw danger approaching and sounded the alarm, the citizens of the town would have time to prepare to defend themselves. If the sentry saw danger approaching and didn't sound the alarm, the blood of the people would be on his head. If the watchman sounded the alarm and the people didn't respond, the blood of the people would be on their own heads. In other words, if the people were warned but chose not to respond, it was their own fault.

Part of the watchman's responsibility was to try and discern the strength of the approaching forces—how many soldiers they had, whether they were on foot or horseback, and whether they had catapults or other destructive weapons. That way the defenders could evaluate their chances for victory, or prepare for surrender. Perhaps a zealous watchman occasionally sounded the alarm only to discover the cloud of dust on the horizon was caused by a caravan of merchants coming to trade in the city. In those instances, he may have had egg on his face, but the safety of the city was nevertheless preserved.

Nobody who has looked seriously at Y2K would say the cloud of dust on the horizon is insignificant, but the size of the approaching

---

What's Ahead

- **New Year's Day, 1999**

- **New Year's Day, 2000**

- **Getting Started on Your Y2K Plan**

37

forces—and their destructive capabilities—is still a matter of debate. Part of the answer, of course, depends on how well prepared the defenders in the city are. If the attacking force is small and poorly equipped, even an unprepared populace will fall more quickly and suffer more painfully than a city that has made some provision. *The essence of provision is looking ahead to supply needs beforehand.*

Because most armies in those days lacked the weaponry to destroy a city's walls, a common tactic was to lay siege and try to starve the defenders out. But if a city had adequate food and water supplies, they could hold out for a long time—often long enough for reinforcements to arrive or for the army to muster and either defeat the enemy or convince them to abandon the siege. If an attacking army was able to cut off the water supply by damming a river, or cut off the food supply by pillaging surrounding farmland, the city was often quick to fall.

Another question to be considered was how long the attacking army could sustain a siege. A few days? A month? A year or more? Again, the answer lay with how well the city had prepared.

In the same way, the key questions swirling around Y2K are, "How long, how severe, and how widespread will the problem be?" No one can answer that with certainty, but our recommendation is that you develop a plan for a short-term, mid-term, or long-term crisis—you can decide for yourself which level of preparedness is most appropriate for your family.

New Year's Day, 1999

If the lights had flickered and gone out on New Year's Day, 1999, you might have been irritated and inconvenienced, and you might have wondered, "How long is this going to last?" More than likely, you would not have panicked, because you would have assumed the problem was local and the power company had technicians deployed to solve the problem and restore service as soon as possible. If the blackout occurred during a storm, you would have known that many lines might be affected and that it would probably take time for your power to come back on. But you still would have expected the duration of the blackout to be measured in minutes or hours.

In extreme cases, you might have tolerated a day or two of outage before you became concerned. As a society, we have a high level of confidence in our utility companies because the level of service they supply is normally quite high and we know that most power outages are due to physical causes that can be remedied relatively quickly, such as when a branch falls on a transmission line or a transformer is struck by lightning.

If you had gone to your bank on Friday, January 2, this year and your ATM card had not worked in the machine, you might have stepped inside the bank to complain, but you would have expected a logical explanation—"Our machines are down" or "Your account is overdrawn." You wouldn't have panicked; you've faced similar problems in the past.

If you picked up the telephone on January 3 and didn't get a dial tone, you would blame the local phone company and try your call again later. Unless your business was dependent on immediate phone service, you probably wouldn't be overly concerned by a brief disruption in service. If the phone was working and you called to make an airline reservation or to resolve a question on your credit-card bill, you wouldn't be surprised to be put on hold. In fact, you would wait on hold until someone came on the line, or simply hang up and plan to call back in an hour. Your blood pressure might climb a few points, but it wouldn't be the end of the world. Accidents happen. Eventually the trouble will be resolved.

New Year's Day, 2000

Flash forward to New Year's Day, Y2K. If the lights go out shortly after midnight on January 1, you will be face-to-face with a new level of uncertainty. Did a tree limb fall on a power line nearby, or has the dreaded Y2K wolf arrived at the door as predicted? As you sit in the dark, will you be wishing you would have planned ahead, or will you be implementing phase one of your emergency plan? If you wait until January 1, it will be too late to formulate a plan. *Today is the day to make that decision.*

You pick up the phone to call your mother, but the line is dead—no dial tone. A tiny seed of panic sprouts in the pit of your stomach. "They'll get it fixed," you mutter to yourself. After all, it isn't the first time you've had a problem with telephone service.

Let's assume the "mission-critical" strategy employed by your local utility company works, and they restore power to your neighborhood by Monday, January 3. Your first trip would be to the bank to get the cash you had intended to withdraw last Friday. When you turn the ignition key on your two-year-old sport utility vehicle, the car won't start. The "check engine" light comes on and stays on, and you decide to walk to the bank.

Surprisingly, there is no line out in front. You insert your ATM card, and the machine swallows it. Now what do you do? Glancing at your watch, you decide to wait for the bank to open. At 9:45 a security guard arrives and announces the bank's opening will be delayed until the manager solves a time-lock problem with the vault, so you decide to come back later. Later that same day, phone service has been restored, but all circuits are busy. You tune in the news on the radio, and the airwaves are humming with reports about Y2K, though nobody seems to know the extent of the problem.

Let's face it: On January 1, 2000, the picture may not be much clearer than it is today. Events in life unfold moment by moment, hour by hour, day by day. Y2K will be no exception. Uncertainty will be the order of the day. If complications occur as predicted, rumors will no doubt multiply about when this service or that system will be restored. Some information will be true; other information will be wishful thinking. Having a well-reasoned plan in place will allow you to deal with the uncertainty constructively.

If the power goes out, you won't know whether the blackout will last hours, days, or even weeks. The more important question is, "Will you be prepared?" If you have food and water and can heat your home, you can survive comfortably for several days. With a more comprehensive plan in place, you can be confident your needs will be at least minimally met for longer. The key will be to have a contingency plan already established.

Getting Started on Your Y2K Plan

Our approach to a Y2K family survival plan is based on several premises. First, it's already too late for many preparation options—*so your plan has to work in the time left before January 1*. Second, most people do not have the option to relocate—*so your plan has to work where you are*. Third, most families have limited resources to utilize in preparation—*so your plan has to be affordable*. Fourth, the ultimate impact of Y2K is uncertain—*so your plan must be flexible* in order to prepare you for a multitude of contingencies. Fifth, circumstances vary—*so your plan must be customized to fit your specific situation*. For example, if you live in the Frost Belt, heat may be your number-one priority after food and water. If you live in the Sun Belt, heat is less of a problem, but waste disposal might be a bigger issue.

Circumstances may vary from place to place. Medical problems, financial decisions, size of household, levels of preparedness, and proximity to urban or rural resources may be different for you than for your neighbors. Access to water, septic tanks, and sewage disposal may become important factors you'll need to consider. Preparing for Y2K is much like preparing for any natural disaster.

The frequency and severity of weather-related disasters seem to have been on the rise for the past several years—perhaps an early warning to motivate us to action. Within recent memory, we've seen an earthquake in Armenia accompanied by terrible snow, floods in China, monsoons in Bangladesh, mud slides in Honduras, a weather-related power blackout in Canada that took experts from across the country almost two weeks to repair, and an assortment of tornadoes, hurricanes, and tropical storms here in the United States. When Hurricane Mitch devastated Central America, relief organizations in the United

States mobilized to collect and distribute emergency-relief supplies, food, and clothing to those who had suffered loss.

But what if the devastation hadn't been caused by a natural disaster in a localized region of the world? What if the need for emergency food, shelter, clothing, and heat were simultaneous worldwide? What if the disaster struck in the middle of winter, as Y2K will in the northern hemisphere? And what if the power, transportation, and communications systems worldwide were shut down or seriously hampered? Who would gather the food and supplies? How would they be delivered? And how would we know where the need is greatest? The global community could very quickly boil down to a world of localized communities, each making the best of the local resources to cope with the problems. Such a scenario would be bad news for the unprepared. That's why it is important to take precautions today, to avoid or at least mitigate a disaster in 2000.

It would be unfair for us to sell you this book without explaining our own preparations, so throughout the book we will offer not only expert recommendations, but our own personal choices regarding surviving Y2K. Some doomsayers have suggested the Y2K bug will bring an end to society as we know it, moving us back about 100 years to the days of the Old West, when it was "every man for himself" and local authorities superseded the federal government's control. Others suggest Y2K will be nothing—a speed bump on the highway of history. The truth is probably somewhere in the middle. So while we are about to offer three scenarios for survival—a two-to-three day plan, a one-month plan, and a one-year plan—you should know that your authors are personally preparing for a month or more of difficulties. That is, we think some glitches will be worked out within the first few days, while other problems will persist for a year or longer. It is almost certain countries in Asia will be hard-hit, and that will no doubt create financial disturbances in the United States. However, we also believe in American ingenuity and in our unique ability to adapt and survive hard times. More than that, we believe most Americans will want to get things going again in this country and will work overtime to reestablish many of the things we've come to take for granted—like television, telephone connections, and the speedy resumption of commerce. And we believe in the gracious providence of God.

With that in mind, each of us is making plans and taking practical steps to face the problems of Y2K, keeping our families safe and warm, and investing in some items we think will smooth the transition. As you read the coming pages, you'll discover what we've found, and we'll share the choices and decisions we have made for our own personal survival. Each chapter that follows will explore a different element of preparedness, such as food storage, finding water, generating heat and light where there is no electricity, what to do about money if the banks fail, and so on. Again, the most important thing we can do is put our faith in God, trusting Him for our future. But we also encourage you to take practical steps to help your family survive in that future world. With most problems in life, if you can't get it done today you can always solve it tomorrow. With Y2K, we know when and where it's going to hit, so the time and place to begin preparing solutions is here and now.

PART TWO

PREPARING YOURSELF

FOUR

First Things First

Procrastination and denial are the two biggest obstacles to preventive preparation. It's easy for us to say, "I don't have time to deal with this now, but I'll get to it as soon as possible." However, unlike other potential disasters, we know *exactly* when Y2K will happen. The time is clearly defined: January 1, 2000. That's helpful in a way, but it can create a false sense of security, tempting us to put off preparation until we're close to the end of 1999. We strongly suggest that the seriousness of potential disaster requires attention now.

As we've already stated, the first step in getting ourselves ready to face the trauma of Y2K is to realize there is a problem and that it might have severe outcomes. But realization requires more than merely thinking about what might happen. We need to handle the problem as though it is a real one—a clear and present danger for which we take practical steps, not just a mental process we think through. What will we need to buy, store, and have on hand if we are to survive Y2K? Perhaps you'll find it helpful to wake yourself up by discovering how dependent we have become on modern conveniences.

What's Ahead

- **An Emergency Test Day**
- **Creating Your Survival Plan**
- **Personal Items**
- **Tool Time**
- **Important Utensils**
- **Making Plans**
- **Your Y2K Planning Guide**

An Emergency Test Day

Remember that Y2K starts on a national holiday, which happens to fall on a Saturday. We can use that to our advantage by arranging our own "emergency test day" sometime this year. Try this exercise: *Set aside one Saturday to prepare for Y2K, making the choice to survive without electricity, gas, water from your faucets, and phones.* You are allowed the convenience of using a weekend for this experiment so you won't lose a workday. In order for this to be effective, your entire family must take part in this exercise. You are trying to understand the impact of not having your normal comforts—in a real crisis this is how everyone will live.

On this day you will not use anything that requires electricity. Unplug your washer, your dryer, your stove, and all your other electrical appliances. Make sure to unplug your clocks, too, so you cannot easily tell time. You can keep the refrigerator and freezer running (after all, this is a test and we don't want you to spoil your food), but you can't use anything in the refrigerator—assume it is spoiled. If you can't use your refrigerator to chill things, and you can't use your stove or microwave to heat them, what will you eat? What will the members of your family prepare for dinner? You can't even use the electric can opener to open the tuna. What do you have on your shelves that can be eaten without preparation?

Since electricity is needed to pump water, your water supply will be limited if not terminated. For the purposes of our test, go to your main water source and turn off your water. With the water shut off, you will not be able to bathe, do your laundry, wash dishes, or flush the toilet. If your food preparation depends on adding water, what will be your water source?

In addition, realize that your loss of electricity will affect your heat and air-conditioning. Even though you might heat your home with gas or oil, more than likely the thermostat is an electric one, so chances are it won't be working after January 1. For the purposes of this test day, turn off your heat and air-conditioning. Obviously, if you are doing this exercise in the warm months it won't mean much, but understand that Y2K begins in the dead of winter. You'll need an alternative energy source for both heat and light. People who live in many western and southern states won't be significantly affected by the loss of heat in the winter months, but if the Y2K problem were to continue into the summer they would certainly feel the loss of their air-conditioning.

One of the effects of a major computer malfunction that concerns the business world is loss of communications equipment, so on your test day you will not use your telephone. Either turn your ringer off so that you can't hear it, or let your answering machine take messages for you all day. If you want a real test, don't rely on the answering machine—disconnect your phone and see what it's like to be out of touch with the world. And don't use your cell phone, e-mail, or fax machine, since all of them will probably fail to work after January 1.

Another area that concerns the business community is transportation—no one knows how the embedded microchips in cars, trucks, and buses will react after Y2K. Therefore, on your test day assume you can't use any form of public transportation. In addition, if you have a newer automobile, don't rely on it working. If your car was manufactured before 1993 it can probably be used because it doesn't have many embedded chips, but if it was made within the last five years, assume it is not Y2K compliant. (To be fair, cars manufactured in 1998 are supposed to be compliant, but testing of all microprocessors has not been completed; therefore, we don't know if new cars will work or not.) For the purposes of our emergency test day, most of us should limit our transportation to walking or cycling.

One final area will involve your money. Even if your bank is open on the test day, pretend it is closed. Imagine that all bank machines don't work, local stores are without power for their cash registers, and no one can validate your credit cards. You can only use the cash you have on you. Again, make this apply to everyone in your family. How would your family operate under these conditions? Spend the day living like this— no television, no radio, no phone calls, no video games, no lights, no heat, and no water. At the end of the day, sit together as a family and discuss what you learned. Does everyone think they could survive like this for a month?

Obviously, if there are any real emergencies that day, you will need to stop the exercise and take care of the situation, but do realize that medical emergencies can and do happen during real disasters. Ask yourself what you would do if you couldn't telephone for an ambulance, contact the police, or call a fire truck. What would happen if your car refused to work and you needed to get to the hospital? Lest you think we're being alarmists, remember that these are exactly the problems that experts believe we will face during the first weekend in the year 2000.

We really hope you'll run through this exercise in order to get a feel for living with Y2K. Even if you don't make it for more than eight hours without giving in and raiding the refrigerator or taking a shower or turning on the television, you will begin to understand the severity of the problem. We all depend on our culture's modern conveniences. For most baby boomers and their children, we only experience separation from modern life when we go on a camping trip . . . and even then how "rough" are we "roughing it"?

Creating Your Survival Plan

Once you comprehend the depth of the problem, your next step is to begin preparing for a real emergency. This is where you begin to create checklists and gather supplies so that you'll have some kind of plan in place—one that can be used for Y2K, earthquakes, hurricanes, or other severe troubles. Even if the Y2K reality turns out to be a minor irritation, the very fact you have prepared will offer benefits for natural or man-made disasters.

We suggest you sit down with your family or friends and brainstorm a plan. Begin to ask yourself and your family some questions:

- What needs to be done?
- What do we need and don't have?
- What do we have now that we can use?
- What will we need to purchase and store?
- How long will we need to plan for?
- Where will we stockpile supplies?
- What alternatives can we brainstorm?
- How much money are we willing to invest in this plan?
- Who will take care of each problem?

We believe it is important for you to make a decision as a family as to how serious you think Y2K will be. If you expect it will create some minor glitches for a week or so, you can create a plan with that in mind. On the other hand, if you think we are more likely to experience problems for a month or more, your family can plan accordingly. And if you are one of those who believes the troubles could last a year or longer, that will cause you to establish an entirely different plan for helping your family survive.

To put the plan into action, it will be helpful if tasks are assigned to various family members. Perhaps one person can be in charge of transportation and communication alternatives, another person will coordinate food and water supplies, and another medical and safety supplies. If you have children, involve them in the process. Even young kids can be made part of the process if we give clear directions and offer some guidance to help them get started. Above all, write things down, so that you have a record and can keep track of your progress.

Once you have an overview of the problem, you will begin to take each area of concern and figure out what to do about it. The rest of this book will help you address the particular concerns and begin to create solutions.

Personal Items

Let us begin with personal items: *What do you need for personal well-being in order to survive?* Each person in your family or circle of friends must answer this question and compile a list.

We'll make some suggestions momentarily, but they are only ideas, and there may be certain things your family needs that we didn't consider. You might simply walk through your house and start thinking about what you would need to do to maintain your family life without any utilities. If you have children, give each child the responsibility of making his or her own personal list. If they know they will have to be responsible for their own things, they are far more likely to be involved with the preparation, and they won't blame you when they realize they forgot something important. (Of course, you may need to help them by editing their lists, especially if they get too long!) Here are some basic personal items you'll want to have handy:

1. *Storage containers*. Each person will need a storage container, or perhaps several containers. You might use old suitcases, heavy plastic cartons, or even cedar blanket boxes. Make sure they are in good condition and will keep moisture and pests out. Some people will use old chests, stainless steel truck boxes, or foot lockers. We encourage people to invest in large Rubbermaid plastic storable chests, which can be stacked inside each other when not in use, thus saving valuable storage space. Be wary of storing anything of value in cardboard boxes—they are susceptible to moisture, and mice can chew through them, getting to your valuables inside.

2. *Clothes*. Each person in your family should have an adequate supply of outerwear like jackets, coveralls, sweaters, sweatpants, and other kinds of warm clothing appropriate for your location. If your children are growing, invest in some jeans and sweatshirts they can grow into. You might also consider purchasing some quality rain gear, since you can count on being out-of-doors during the long winter months. In parts of the United States, January and February are very cold months, and you may be facing the prospect of regularly walking to your destinations, so protection from snow and rain is essential. In addition to outerwear, think about the casual clothing you will need. If you were unable to purchase shirts, pants, underwear, and socks for several months, how much would your family need on

hand? If you live in apart of the country that needs hats, gloves, and thermal underwear during the winter, make sure you stock up—every expert agrees they will be hard to come by in the winter of 2000. Don't forget shoes and boots, and invest in some heavy socks. Finally, you will want to consider sleepwear. Depending on your location and personal comfort, you may want to invest in something that will keep you warm while the heat is off.

Before storing your clothing, make sure the things going into containers fit comfortably. Clean and mend everything before putting it away, and make sure to have needles and thread in your home. In choosing clothes for children, think rugged and outdoorsy. You will also need to consider what you will use to clean these clothes in the event of an extended emergency—laundry soap that works in cold water and plenty of chlorine bleach.

3. *Toiletries.* This includes personal hygiene items such as toothbrushes, floss, toothpaste, hairbrushes, combs, deodorant, mouthwash, and soap. Make sure to store plenty of washcloths and towels, since it may take longer to wash and dry them if your electricity is out for any length of time. Stock up on toilet paper, shaving equipment, and feminine hygiene supplies. If you wear glasses, you may want to have an extra pair available. Vitamins, mineral supplements, and aspirin are going to be important, so purchase extra bottles in bulk. And consider any special medications your family requires—can you get your prescription filled far in advance? What is the shelf life of your medication? If you have special medical needs like insulin or oxygen tanks, talk to your doctor about getting prescriptions for extra supplies.

4. *Bedding.* We recommend having warm sleeping bags for each member of your family. Purchasing additional pillows and blankets is also going to be important. If the prospect of leaving your dwelling for overnight or extended periods of time is a concern, or there is the possibility someone might need to stay with you, we definitely recommend that you have some emergency bedding stored in a dust-free container.

5. *Garbage bags.* Even if the emergency situation lasts only a weekend, you will create garbage. Large plastic garbage bags can be purchased cheaply in bulk, and have hundreds of uses—they can temporarily protect food, store water, keep dust off important items, protect documents from moisture, and even be worn as emergency rain ponchos. Of course, you also need to think about what you will do with the garbage you will generate. Will your trash company be working? Will you bury the garbage you create? What happens if you live in a large apartment building? Plan to burn all paper products, wash and store all plastics, and tightly seal solid waste in plastic garbage bags.

6. *Recreational activities.* If there is no electricity, there will be no television, no VCR, no Nintendo, and perhaps no radio stations operating. How will you keep your family amused? In a real emergency, emotional stress and tension are already factors, so the more you can do to lessen the tension the better. Board games, balls, non-electric toys, and books can be helpful diversions. Talk with your family about what you should do together as a family that doesn't require plugging into a socket.

7. *Pet supplies.* In addition to food for your pets, you will need to determine what toilet, grooming, and medical supplies you might need for them.

8. *Important papers and personal identification.* In later chapters we will examine the need for hard copies of important financial information. The basic rule, however, is simple: If it's important, make a copy now and put it in a protected place. Remember: Y2K is a computer problem, so important financial and real estate information should be recorded on hard copy in case you are asked to prove ownership at some later date. Anticipate problems by safely storing evidence of credit cards, debt, and paid-off loans.

9. *Cash and coins.* ATMs will probably be out of commission during the Y2K crisis, and credit cards may not be helpful if banks cannot communicate electronically with each other. Therefore, having on hand a reasonable amount of hard currency before the end of the year will offer you some peace of

mind. The amount you keep will be determined by what you think you'll need and the degree of security you feel.

10. *Neighborhood information.* If you really want to prepare for Y2K, talk with your family, friends, and neighbors about what they are doing. There is peace of mind in knowing your loved ones are safe and yours is not the only family that has thought about surviving the potential upheavals. Your children need to know who they can go to for help in an emergency, and if you are separated from parents or children, it's imperative you have a plan for contacting them at some point in the future.

Tool Time

In addition to personal items, *you will need to have certain tools and utensils close at hand.* For a two- or three-day crisis, the tools may not be as important, but for an extended emergency situation they will prove invaluable. You will probably have many of these things already, so you may not need to buy them, but you will want to know where they are.

1. *Hand tools.* Every family should have a medium-weight hammer, a staple gun with lots of staples, a standard screwdriver, Phillips screwdrivers of varying sizes, common pliers, wire cutters, a standard-size adjustable crescent wrench, a hacksaw with extra blades, and a crowbar. Note that all these tools are manually operated and not dependent upon batteries or electrical outlets. Electric screwdrivers are a great convenience, but if they have no power they'll be more awkward to use than conventional ones.

2. *Cutting tools.* If your heating fuel is wood, you will need to have such things as a good rough-cut handsaw, an ax, and a hatchet. Keep these sharpened and out of the reach of children. You will also want a whetstone and a pocketknife (ideally, one that has several different kinds of blades like a Swiss Army knife.) A good pair of sharp fabric scissors can be added to your list as well.

3. *Digging tools.* These tools are necessary for an extended crisis: a shovel, hoe, and pickax. They will be used for helping

eliminate garbage and sewage problems, and possibly for digging an outdoor fire pit. An Army trenching tool is ideal because it works as both a shovel and pickax, and a posthole digger can be useful if it becomes necessary to make an outhouse or build a fence.

4. *Twine, baling wire, caulking, and duct tape.* During an extended emergency, it may be necessary to build small structures or repair damage on your home. These supplies will come in handy for fixing any number of problems.

5. *Nails of different sizes.* We suggest an assortment of nails to meet the needs of a variety of projects. Buy them in bulk, not small packages, and store them by size in containers with lids to keep them dry.

6. *Tarps and plastic bags.* These can be used for storage, protection, and temporary cover, if required. Buy large sizes at outdoor supply stores, and keep them in a place where they are easy to access.

7. *Batteries.* Have a supply of long-lasting batteries in different sizes. Flashlights, lamps, fire detectors, and radios can last a long time on one battery, but make sure to spend the extra money on good-quality, long-life batteries. Rechargeable batteries are not recommended because of the unpredictable nature of the electrical power supply.

8. *Fuels for lanterns, cookstoves, and generators.* Many people who have purchased generators have forgotten that without abundant fuel, their generator is worthless. If you plan to rely on a camp stove, buy an extra tank of propane and fill it early in 1999. Be very careful when storing these kinds of items—if possible, keep them outside in a locked shed. Candles and kerosene will prove valuable, but be careful—many Americans have forgotten how to use them safely. If you can use alternatives and cut down on your need for kerosene and gasoline, do so.

9. *Work gloves and goggles.* Like many of the above items, these will not be required for a two- or three-day emergency, but for an extended crisis, safety goggles and work gloves will help protect your eyes and hands. Work injuries during a national emergency could lead to disaster.

10. *Matches and lighters.* Friends of ours once felt totally prepared for a blizzard, having stored up paper, wood, candles, and kerosene lamps. Unfortunately, once the snow was on the ground they realized they had only one book of matches with them. Protect your family by having an adequate supply of matches and lighters, and keep in mind that matches are like frozen food, having a shelf life of little more than a year.

Important Utensils

All of the above tools will be necessary to use in case of a Y2K emergency. You should also consider this list of important utensils to have on hand:

1. *Eating and cooking utensils.* More than likely you will already have all the utensils you would normally need for eating and cooking—plates, glasses, and flatware. However, keep in mind that electrical appliances such as toasters, coffeemakers, microwaves, and can openers won't work. You will need to invest in cooking items that are either manually operated or use other sources of fuel. Cooking can be done on a camp stove fueled by propane, in a barbecue, or in a fire pit in your backyard. Remember that you might need special pots and pans, since your nice copper pans aren't usable in your gas barbecue.

2. *Fire extinguishers.* Cooking fires, kerosene lanterns, improperly stored gas, and camp stoves are all fire hazards. Invest in some fresh fire extinguishers, make sure they have an adequate ABC rating, and teach your children how to use them properly. In addition to an extinguisher, you may want to consider having small cans of sand to smother fires.

3. *Plastic or metal basins.* You will need something to wash yourself and your dishes. Dish soap, sponges, washrags, and towels are necessary, because your dishwasher will be out of commission. A good-sized metal bowl will be priceless for heating water on a fire or wood stove and taking a sponge bath.

4. *Light sources.* Have a healthy supply of candles and flashlights. You may want to check out battery-operated lamps, kerosene lanterns, or propane torches. Make sure to invest in

long-life batteries, spare bulbs, and waterproof matches. Talk with your children about the safe use of open-flame light sources, so they know what to do in an emergency.

5. *Transistor radio.* For a short-term emergency, a transistor radio will be a practical item to have. Again, invest in an extra supply of batteries, and try not to overuse the radio and wear down the batteries too quickly.

6. *Portable toilet.* During sustained power outages, solid waste has proven to be one of the greatest problems. Invest in a good quality chemical camp toilet. For single individuals and small families, a portable toilet with plastic bags will probably work fine for a limited period of time. For extended periods or for larger families, an outhouse or outdoor toilet of some kind will need to be dug.

7. *Bicycles.* Although not absolutely necessary, a bicycle can be a very nice thing to have during an extended emergency. If we can't rely on our cars, public transportation, or working streetlights, bicycles will at least allow us to get around quickly and conveniently. Keep a tire pump and extra tires or a patch kit on hand.

8. *A basic first-aid kit.* In a later chapter we will detail the requirements for a good, reliable medical kit, but for now you should recognize the importance of handling cuts, pain, and contusions with common sense and a few handy supplies. Complete kits can be purchased at any drugstore, or you can make your own. You will also want to invest in a medical book to handle possible injuries and illnesses.

9. *Writing materials.* Paper, pencils, pens, and indelible markers will be invaluable for making lists, writing messages, and making warning signs. They will also help your children pass the time and continue their education if the schools do not immediately reopen.

10. *Jugs and containers.* In the next two chapters we will discuss food and water supplies, but for the moment we'll remind you that water is the most important ingredient for your family's survival. Stocking up now on safe containers for water storage is

essential, since nearly every water company has predicted a shortage of large-quantity water jugs by late 1999.

Making Plans

When you give yourself a test of a weekend without electricity, water, and other necessities, you will discover what sort of plan your family needs to make in order to survive Y2K. The difference between surviving and thriving is preparation—an emergency becomes less traumatic the more we prepare for it. We strongly recommend you practice with an emergency test day. Try it just one day, and you'll see how you fare. The practice session is itself a form of preparation. You will know better what you need, what you can do to prepare, and what will happen if you actually go through the procedures. Even if Y2K turns out to be a slight annoyance rather than a prolonged disaster, you will now be prepared for other emergency situations.

Much of what we are calling an emergency situation is really more a circumstance creating discomfort than threatening a life. In many areas of the world these unfortunate and uncomfortable conditions are part of the daily routine. We late-twentieth-century Americans have become spoiled with luxuries and have begun to think of telephones and televisions as "necessities." We not only want our MTV, we expect it. Our grandparents and great-grandparents certainly didn't enjoy the lifestyles most of us do these days, yet they survived very well. You can too.

We're not criticizing our modern lifestyle, only reminding you that some of the things we live with are not essential to survival. Even if we need to temporarily give up our computers, televisions, CD players, and other wonderful devices, we still have technologies that didn't exist at the beginning of this century. Let us not forget the pioneering spirit that is the foundation of this country. Our forefathers dealt with all manner of troubles and life-threatening circumstances, and managed to not only survive but create the greatest nation on earth. We believe we can definitely conquer this potential problem.

Preparing ourselves materially and mentally will enable us to do so.

One of the factors in getting ready for Y2K is to speculate how long we will need to endure the crisis. You may have noticed that some of the items listed above were more suited for an extended period of time. Even though the beginning date is clearly defined, the degree and duration of the problem is something we really don't know. The longer the length of time you think we'll have trouble, the more extensive your planning needs to be. Start thinking about what time period your family will want to prepare for. Certainly it is far easier to plan for a two- or three-day emergency than a yearlong emergency—and you'll find most commercially available survival kits are based on a 72-hour emergency scenario.

However, *we suggest 72 hours be the minimum amount of time you are prepared to face.* Factors affecting your preparation will be expense, time, space, and your attitude. If your budget is tight, spending 200 dollars on a survival kit for each person in the family may be unreasonable. If you live in a studio apartment, having space to store a year's supply of survival goods is unlikely. If you are a single parent working full-time and raising two children, finding the time to plan for an emergency will be difficult. These elements will affect your attitude. Your perspective and beliefs about the seriousness of Y2K will determine what you decide to do. Wisdom says we should take reasonable precautions, so our recommendation is clear: Prepare for as long a period of time as you can.

Your Y2K Planning Guide

Personal Items to Have on Hand

1. Plenty of storage containers.
2. Warm clothes, with sizes for children to grow into, and means for washing them.
3. Toiletries, including toothbrushes, toilet paper, and feminine-hygiene supplies.
4. Sleeping bags, bedding, and extra blankets.
5. Garbage bags.
6. Games and recreational activities.
7. Pet supplies.
8. Copies of important papers and personal identification.
9. An adequate supply of cash and coins.
10. Neighborhood information.

Tools

1. Hand tools, including hammer, staple gun, screwdrivers, pliers, wire cutters, crescent wrench, hacksaw, and crowbar.
2. Cutting tools, including handsaw, ax, hatchet, scissors, and a Swiss army knife.
3. Digging tools, including shovel, hoe, and pickax.
4. Twine, baling wire, caulking, and duct tape.
5. Nails of different sizes.
6. Tarps and plastic bags.
7. A large supply of batteries.
8. Fuels for lanterns, cook stoves, and generators.
9. Work gloves and goggles.
10. Matches and lighters.

Utensils

1. Eating and cooking utensils, including a stove and heat source.
2. Fire extinguishers.
3. Plastic or metal basins.
4. Light sources such as candles, flashlights, battery-operated lamps, kerosene lanterns, or propane torches.
5. Transistor radio.
6. Portable toilet.
7. Bicycles.
8. A basic first-aid kit.
9. Writing materials.
10. Jugs and containers for drinking water.

FIVE

Stocking the Shelves

W hat did you have for dinner last night? Did you prepare it yourself or did you order pizza? If you did prepare dinner, did you buy the ingredients on the way home from work? Did you really cook dinner, or did you heat it up in the microwave?

For many Americans, cooking a meal is something reserved for the weekends or holidays. We rarely plan meals more than a day in advance, and rely heavily on the convenience of supermarkets having what we need when we need it. Many people depend upon fast-food restaurants to supply a large portion of the meals they eat. How we eat and how we buy has influenced the supermarket and restaurant industries. Many grocery stores and restaurants base their inventory on quick turnaround. Computer programs help them manage the stock and predict demands on their inventory. Y2K will certainly have its impact upon those stores and restaurants that do not have Y2K-compliant systems. Date-sensitive information, such as expiration dates that pass 1999 on foodstuffs, will cause computer problems. Knowing this potential outcome, large corporate restaurant chains and supermarkets are working to make their software Y2K compliant, but that's not the only consideration.

What's Ahead

- **Storage**

- **The Two- to Three-Day Plan**

- **The One-Month Plan**

- **The One-Year Plan**

- **Your Y2K Planning Guide**

Concerns about waste and spoilage are the major reasons behind the practice of keeping low inventories. Expectations of a plentiful supply and quick delivery have created a dependency the retailers base their supply tactics on. Therefore the problem is not simply if your local grocer's computer can deal with Y2K products. What happens if the delivery system fails?

If freight trains and trucks can't deliver the food to the stores, then restocking becomes impossible. It really doesn't matter if the supply is out there somewhere; what matters is whether it gets to its final destination. Have you ever gone to the store to get something and discovered the item was temporarily out? If Y2K cripples transportation, that frustration could be felt by millions of Americans. Disappointment at not having your favorite Oreo cookies is one thing, but real hunger caused by lack of food supply is an entirely different and more sobering issue.

Here's a simple test: Go to your kitchen right now and check out your current stock of food. Ask yourself if you have enough food to eat reasonably well for the next two days without buying anything more. Now take away any items that require refrigeration or cooking. Granted, refrigerated items won't spoil immediately, but many things won't keep more than a day. Perishable foods kept at room temperature for more than two hours are unsafe to eat. In addition, not all refrigerated items need to be cooked. So you could use some of those things and be all right, but a week-long crisis without electricity would definitely cause spoilage and limit cooking. For the sake of this exercise, count only those foodstuffs that need no cooking or refrigeration. How would you do? The result of this test will give you a very rough idea of how prepared you are for a short-lived emergency.

Now think a bit longer term: You may be able to handle the inconvenience of two or three days without additional food, but how would you do for a month? A year? The purpose of this chapter is to help you prepare for all three possibilities. Before we start stocking our shelves, we need to consider how we are going to store our food.

Storage

Your storage will be affected by the number of people in your family, the amount of space you have available, the length of time for which you are planning, and the particular requirements of the food items you select. Six people living in a four-bedroom house will have different storage needs than a single person living in a studio apartment. The family of six will need a lot of food even for two or three days, though this is usually offset by available storage space. The individual will not need as much space for storing a smaller amount of food, but he or she will have less space available to store things. Put the six people in the studio apartment and you have some real problems.

You need to plan for food storage. First, decide how many people are involved. Second, consider the daily requirements for each person in your family. Take into consideration special diets based on allergic reactions and other medical conditions— a six-year-old girl will probably eat a lot less food than a sixteen-year-old boy. Third, determine the amount of time you are preparing for. As we noted earlier, the longer the amount of time you can provide for, the better. These considerations will help to determine how much you are going to store. Once you have a rough idea, you can deduce how much space it will require.

For a single person, a carefully packed plastic carton, 16 x 11x 13 inches, might hold enough for several days. Canned and dried foods that require little or no water for preparation are ideal. This carton can be placed under a bed or in a closet— you'll want a cool, dry area to store your goods. A spare cabinet in the kitchen might be reserved for emergency stores only. If you are planning food storage for a big family, start dedicating space in a garage, closet, shed, or bedroom. As long as the provisions are sealed in a dry, protected place, they should be safe.

People who live in areas of the country where weather-related emergencies are common will know approximately how much food to store, and in fact may already have stored enough food for a three-day family emergency. As we discuss longer periods of time, we will examine other forms of storage such as root cellars and straw boxes.

The Two- to Three-Day Plan

We will assume there is no electricity and you don't have a propane refrigerator. *You will rely solely on food that can be stored in a cool, dry place.* Some examples of foods that do not need to be heated include canned juice, freeze-dried foods, nuts, high-protein bars, crackers, peanut butter, powdered milk, Jell-O (only the prepared snack kind doesn't need heating), instant pudding, dry cereals, and dried fruit such as raisins, prunes, and apricots. If you have a small camp stove, some foods that might require hot water would include packaged soups, canned beans, canned chili, canned stew, coffee, tea, instant cocoa, and canned meat. You might want to add flour, sugar, rice, dried beans, salt, pepper, baking soda, baking powder, herbs, and spices. Don't forget pet food if you need it.

Getting together enough food for three days isn't really much of a problem. It's not terribly expensive and doesn't require much space; however, this isn't a task you want to put off until December 1999. It's possible by that time many people will have begun to worry and started stockpiling foodstuffs. It may not be possible at that late date to find many of the foods you like.

Sometime soon, sit down with the members of your family and plan a three-day "disaster menu." You might even work out what will be the breakfast on day one, then on day two, and so on. Of course, you don't need to be that specific, but you do need to consider how many meals you intend to have. Realize it's not necessary for a human being to have three full meals a day—a good breakfast and an early dinner are really sufficient. You might want to add some snacks like dried fruit instead of planning a big lunch.

It is important to have a wide variety of foods your family actually likes. You can buy commercially prepared survival kits, but do you really want to eat those foods? They may be nutritionally sound, but are often fairly tasteless. Children especially may not like the textureless food in aluminum packets. Make sure the foods you store will keep for at least six months, then restock as needed.

In a short-term emergency, it may be quite likely you will not need to heat any of the foods you eat. However, you might want to have hot foods, especially if you are in the colder parts of the country. This means you need to have some way to cook your food. Remember, we are assuming your electricity is out, so you can't use the microwave or an electric stove. It's possible a gas stove will still work, though that depends on your utility company having generators to pump the gas through the lines. Our recommendation is that you invest in a portable camp stove which works on propane, cooking outside or on a porch, and having it available for your family camping trips. Keep in mind you'll need fuel for your stove, so plan to purchase an extra propane tank and have it filled early in 1999. A gas barbecue will work well for a short-term problem, though it won't be nearly as flexible if the Y2K troubles extend for a month or more.

If your dwelling has a working fireplace, you might be able to cook on it. However, cooking in a fireplace is not the easiest thing to do, and it's hard on your pots and pans, so you may want to experiment to see how to do it. Under no circumstances should you cook over compressed fire logs—they generally contain harmful fumes that will contaminate your food. If your home has a wood stove or fireplace insert, you may be able to cook on the top surface, or at least heat water on it.

If you live in the country or in a house with a backyard, you have another possible alternative: the fire pit. There are basically two kinds of fire pits—above-ground and below-ground. The below-ground pit is easiest to make. Simply dig a trench about a 12 inches deep, 18 inches wide, and 18 or more inches long. Into this trench you pile wood and set it on fire. Once the flames are down, you are left with great burning embers. By placing a rack from your electric oven or barbecue grill over the pit, you can cook any number of foods. With a heavy covered pot like a Dutch oven you can even bake bread and make casseroles.

An above-ground fire pit can be formed out of bricks and stones. Scoop out a little bit of the earth and make a circular or rectangular pit, then build your fire in the center, placing the rack on top of the bricks. Any size of pit can be built as long as the bricks or blocks are a uniform size. A deep, large pit will be useful for boiling water. The advantage of the below-ground pit is that it's very easy to make and contains the fire a bit better.

The One-Month Plan

A supply of food for a month requires extensive planning of what you want to store and what amounts you will want to have. Ready-to-eat canned meals might be OK for two days, but they are expensive, and over time you will need to think about making and cooking more enjoyable meals for your family. You will want to store such things as flour, sugar, rice, dried beans, salt, pepper, baking soda, baking powder, herbs, and spices. You'll also want to add vegetable or olive oil to your stores. *It's helpful if you work out a tentative month-long menu, so that you buy adequate quantities with enough variation.* Realize the restrictions you are working with and find meals that fit those particular restrictions yet are still tasty and nutritious.

We keep mentioning dried and canned foods as possibilities. Certainly you can buy such things from the grocery store, but it is also possible and inexpensive (and even fun) to make your own. Canning is something many baby boomers will remember their parents doing, and may have even done themselves. The equipment needed is inexpensive, and once purchased, it will last a long time. The only thing you'll need to replace are the canning lids, since the jars can be used repeatedly. If you are thinking about doing your own canning, make sure you have a good supply of new lids and rings.

You can also dry your own foods, especially fruit and vegetables. The most dependable tool for drying is a dehydrator. Like the canning equipment, once the investment is made you have a device that will last a long time. It is also possible to sun-dry food; it merely requires a screen and a sunny climate. You can also use a warm oven with an open door (for ventilation) to dry food. Store the dried foods in jars or plastic zip-lock bags. If you use bags, be aware that such bags are not rodent proof, so you'll want to put them into a tightly lidded metal container. Having your own garden will help keep costs down and put healthy food on your plate. Buying in bulk (or buying in bulk with friends) will also help lower your costs.

Granted, preparing for a month will definitely require more thinking, more space, and more money, but we believe in the long run it might be very beneficial to be that prepared. One way to reduce costs is to buy bulk foods from discount restau-rant-supply houses like Price-Costco or Sam's Club. If there is a minimal Y2K crisis, you will still have a general supply for other emergencies—admittedly a wise thing.

If you believe Y2K is going to cause problems for a month or longer, your food storage plan will have to grow and change. Storing food for a month-long emergency requires more plan-ning, more space, and more money. Depending upon the size of your dwelling and the number of people in your family, you might already have enough space to keep a month's supply of food in your garage, closet, or storage space. If you don't, you'll need to create more storage space in your dwelling, and that might mean having a garage sale to get rid of some of those things you don't need or want. Building or purchasing some inexpensive shelving can help you organize your foodstuffs, and arranging them so you can easily get at the food is essential. Many families buy food in bulk and slowly use these stores, replenishing them every three or four months and taking care to rotate the supply so that nothing spoils or goes stale.

Another alternative is to rent storage space somewhere out-side your home. In large cities many apartment dwellers already rent space in a mini-storage facility. This means additional costs for rent and perhaps for building additional shelves, since most of these storage units are unlit, unheated, and bare. It also means transportation of the goods—how will you get the foodstuffs from where you have them stored to where you are living? If there is a month-long crisis, there will be many hungry, desperate people on the streets. You may not want to be walking home and carrying a supply of food. On the other hand, most storage spaces are well-protected with fences and dogs. If you need to rent additional space away from your dwelling, find a facility that is close to you and in a relatively safe area.

For those who live in a house with a yard, there are two other alternatives. One is to build or buy a shed. We know a family that purchased a prefabricated shed, sold as a tool shack, at a very reasonable price. Make sure the shed is leak-proof and lockable. When storing food outdoors, be certain the items are sealed to protect them from insects and vermin. Stack the items well, putting some thought into what will be on top so that you don't have to unpack the entire shed to find what you need.

The other alternative is to use a root cellar—essentially a small, dark, dry storage area dug into the ground. It is not a difficult thing to make, and has proven to be useful over the course of history. You'll need a shovel, some plastic sheeting or garbage bags to line the walls, and some wood pallets. Dig a hole that is at least six feet deep and four feet square. The colder the winters where you live, the deeper the hole should be (make sure it is below the frost line). Wood pallets go on the floor and on all four sides, then the plastic sheeting is tacked or stapled onto the pallets. The last element is a lid, which you want to fit snugly and be at least six inches below ground level. Cover the lid with plastic sheeting, and you've got a poor-man's refrigerator.

What can you store in a root cellar? Vegetables such as turnips, beets, carrots, cabbage, onions, potatoes, and winter squash can be stored in baskets or boxes. The layers of vegetables should be covered with straw. It's best if the vegetables do not touch each other, so packing straw between each one will help to keep them separated. Canned goods and well-sealed dried foods may also be kept in a root cellar. Pack each item carefully to avoid damage.

A final alternative, and one designed to keep items cool, is the straw-box cooler. While not designed for long-term storage, it can still be a helpful thing to have in warm-weather climates. The straw-box cooler consists of two wooden boxes, one fitting inside the other. Between these two boxes place cool, wet straw. The smaller box must be completely covered with moist straw and the lid of the larger box must fit snugly. The result works very similarly to a plastic picnic cooler. If kept in a dark location, it is an ideal way to keep baby formula and insulin from overheating.

The One-Year Plan

If the One-Month Plan seems like a difficult amount of time to imagine a crisis lasting, the One-Year Plan is nearly unfathomable. However, if you were to read some of the potential problems associated with Y2K, a yearlong crisis is not necessarily impossible. There are even Y2K scenarios that involve several years. Planning for a year requires much more storage space and certainly more money. *The cost of food supplies for one person for the One-Year Plan is roughly 700 dollars to 1000 dollars, which means for a family of four the investment is going to be about 4000 dollars!* This amount of food will also demand a lot of space—probably an entire room in your house. In a worst-case scenario, you can even tear open the sheetrock on your walls and store things in the wall space. This degree of preparedness requires a serious commitment, so ask yourself: Are you willing to spend that amount of money and dedicate a room of your living quarters for a potential crisis?

You need to examine your belief in the United States government and the corporate community. Do you believe the federal government will have all or 90 percent of its computers Y2K compliant in time to avert a crippling disaster? Do you trust corporate America to have its systems Y2K compliant in time to avert a catastrophe? If there is a national disaster, will these two institutions be strong enough to survive and help the American public? Knowing your answers to these questions will help you assess the degree to which you want to commit.

To store food items that will last a year or longer, packaging is of the utmost importance. Look for things that are vacuum-packed or freeze-dried. Companies specializing in emergency foods use these kinds of packaging. Commercially available emergency food kits are worth knowing about, but they can be expensive and may be difficult to obtain after March 1999. Most canned items are all right, but they can begin to spoil after a year's time, so check expiration dates. Some foods that will last a year or longer include canned dry whole milk, canned meat, canned condensed vegetable and meat soups, canned stews and chilis, canned fruit, canned dry cereals, and canned dehydrated soups. Other items with a long shelf life include nuts, hard candy, instant pudding, instant cocoa, coffee, tea, dry cream products, bouillon, flavored extracts, baking soda, baking powder, herbs, spices, dried fruit, syrup, peanut butter, jams and jellies, sauces, popcorn, biscuit mix, and pasta.

In recent years consumers have been warned of the dangers of foods packed in plastics. While there is no direct medical evidence it leads to health problems, there is clearly a "leeching" effect of plastic into foods. Therefore most foods should be put in paper bags, and the bags should be placed in plastic. As long as the food is not directly touching the plastic, it remains safe. Meat that has been frozen will stay good a long time as long as your freezer remains closed. However, if a blackout begins to stretch for several days, you may want to cook all your meat so that you can store it.

What amounts of food does one person need to last a year? A single person will need 30 gallons of wheat, 18 gallons of assorted dry beans, 6 gallons of brown rice, 6 gallons of instant milk, 6 gallons of rolled oats, 6 gallons of dried corn, 6 gallons of sugar, one number 10 size can of iodized salt, 36 ounces of yeast, and one gallon of vegetable oil. If you believe that the Y2K problems will last a year or longer there is a good chance you have already considered leaving the city behind and moving further out into the country. If you have even a small area of land, you can grow your own vegetables and other crops. A small orchard is a wonderful thing to have and provides a variety of fruits that can be canned or dried. Of course, where you live will determine what kind of things you plant. Some vegetables require climates of 40 days of 70-degree weather; others require much less. You will need to learn what kinds of things grow well where you live. An herb garden can be easily made with a small amount of space. Even apartment dwellers can grow some vegetables and herbs in window boxes.

Dairy products can be obtained by owning cows or goats. Obviously, this option is not for every family, but milk is an essential part of most American's diets, so consider what your source for milk will be. If you have a backyard and the zoning allows for it, chickens will provide eggs and goats can provide milk—they do not produce the amount of milk cows do, but they are much less expensive to buy and raise.

This is not intended to be a book on farming techniques. There is a lot to know, and we are not recommending everyone run to the country and start their "millennial farm." It's a difficult and sometimes grueling lifestyle which is not suited for many people. But you need to consider the alternatives for your family's survival. Start exploring your beliefs regarding the degree of the Y2K crisis. What you believe will ultimately determine your level of commitment to your survival needs.

Finally, we do not recommend telling people you are storing foods for the long term. Some people will think you've gone off the deep end, others will try to talk you out of it . . . and everyone will keep the information filed away in the back of their minds. If the Y2K problem creates a major crisis, they'll be at your door, asking to take from your supply.

You will also want to have on hand baking powder, bouillon cubes, cocoa powder, cornstarch, garlic, hard candy, nuts, peanut butter, pepper, pickles, raisins, tea, vinegar, vitamins, and yeast. By all means, have a cookbook with which you are comfortable.

You may choose to include pet food, soda pop, and freeze-dried meals (ready-to-eat—called "MREs" by the government). It is important that you plan to rotate these foodstuffs, using them regularly rather than letting them sit a long time.

Obviously, planning for the One-Year Plan simply means increasing the amount you have stored. If you have relatives or friends who might be joining you, consider adding more to your storage.

YOUR Y2K PLANNING GUIDE

A One-Month Food Storage Guide for a Family of Four

40 pounds of potatoes (keep in cool, dry place—away from rodents!)
15 pounds dried beans (buy in bulk, store in five-gallon plastic buckets)
15 pounds dried rice (buy in bulk, store in five-gallon plastic buckets)
15 pounds dried pasta (buy in bulk, store in five-gallon plastic buckets)
90 pounds of fruit (canned, dried, or fresh, stored safely in plastic)
90 pounds of vegetables (canned, dried, or fresh, stored safely)
40 pounds of meat (canned, dried, smoked, or salted, stored in a cool, dry place)
15 pounds of flour (packed in paper bags and stored in plastic buckets)
12 loaves of bread (packed in paper bags and stored safely)
9 gallons of milk (powdered milk can be bought in bulk)
8 pounds of butter (kept cool and dry, butter lasts much longer than margarine)
8 dozen eggs (kept cool, eggs last a very long time)
6 boxes of cornflakes (keep stored in safe container)
6 pounds fresh greens (store in cool, dry place)
5 pounds of oatmeal (buy in bulk, store in five-gallon plastic bucket)
4 pounds of cheese (kept cool and dry, cheese lasts a long time)
4 pounds of coffee (keep stored in safe container)
3 pounds of sugar (buy in bulk, keep in paper bag, store in a plastic bucket)
2 pounds of cornmeal (buy in bulk, keep in paper bag, store safely)
1 pound of salt (store in cool, dry place)
1 gallon of shortening (store in cool, dry place)
Spices (store in cool, dry place)

SIX

Water for a Rainy Day

T hree days without water will kill the average person. It is a vital requirement for life—two quarts of water is the amount an adult should drink each day. Yet we have a tendency to take water for granted, perhaps even abuse our privileges. A shower uses ten gallons of water. The average amount of water used in washing dishes is about five gallons. Running the hot water continually to rinse those dishes can take up to 16 gallons. Forty to fifty gallons are needed to wash one load of clothes. Merely flushing the toilet can use five to seven gallons of water! On any given day, your family uses a lot of water, and they expect water to be there whenever they want it.

Unfortunately, the water industry is one of the biggest users of embedded chips. They are installed in millions of pumping stations, water treatment plants, and sewage works. If those systems are not Y2K compliant, our communities will have a huge problem. Even if the water industry manages to become completely Y2K compliant, it is still reliant on electrical power. If Y2K knocks out the power grid, water cannot be pumped through the pipes. Even if the power grid is not out a long time, there is still the problem of billing. Because of

What's Ahead

- **Storing Water**
- **The Two- to Three-Day Plan**
- **The One-Month Plan**
- **The One-Year Plan**
- **Your Y2K Planning Guide**

computer glitches, your water company might very well think you haven't paid your water bill, and your water service could be terminated.

Those three factors: embedded chips, electric power dependency, and potential billing problems are reasons we need to seriously consider stockpiling water in preparation for Y2K. The amount of water you store will be affected by the same things which influenced food storage: the number of people in your family, the amount of space you have for storage, and the length of time you have left to prepare.

Storing Water

The accepted standard of minimum water need is *one gallon of water per person per day*. So a family of four will need to store four gallons of water for each day. The good news about water storage is we don't really need to spend additional money. The containers can be recycled from other products—plastic soft drink bottles and commercial water bottles. You already have a water source. If flushing the toilet uses five gallons of water, all you need to do is to not flush the toilet once a day and you will save enough water from that action to fill five one-gallon jugs. The only expense you might have is a water filtering system, but that's not totally necessary. Your choice will depend upon the quality of your tap water and how much you trust your utility company.

If you don't stockpile water and there is an emergency, you still have some options. One possibility is to buy water, but that will prove costly, and the supply will be limited. In an emergency situation, water becomes a precious commodity. During the last Bay Area earthquake disaster, water was selling for ten dollars a gallon on the black market.

Another possibility is to rely on the local authorities and emergency organizations like the Red Cross to distribute water. Besides relying on "the government"—something many people are loath to do—this also requires trusting in a good transportation and distribution process. So while your local government might promise you access to clean drinking water, it might take a while to actually get your allotted amount. Not planning for an emergency will put you in the position of needing to depend on this alternative.

Using water you already have is the third possibility. In case you didn't realize it, you have a stockpile of water in your home already. The toilet storage tank has about five gallons of usable water (we are not referring to the toilet bowl, but to the tank). If you have two toilets in your home, you have ten gallons of water. This water is clean and drinkable as long as it doesn't contain a chemical sanitizer. Your water heater contains between 55 and 75 gallons of drinkable water. For two people that's enough water to last three weeks! To access the water from the heater, make sure the gas or electricity is turned off, then turn the valve which lets water into the tank and turn on nearby hot-water faucets. Open the valve at the bottom of the tank, and you can drain all that water into a clean container. Siphon it, if necessary. Filter the water through a cloth to strain out any glass or particles from your water heater. You can even keep rusty water for other purposes, like bathing or washing clothes.

Still another source is the existing water in your pipes. If you shut off your water main before the water stops flowing, you will trap between 10 and 20 gallons of water in the pipes of your home. If you really want to be careful, fill your bathtubs with water late on the night of December 31, 1999. The tub will act as a reservoir, and water can be taken from there and used to wash bodies, dishes, and clothes.

People living in the country will probably have their own wells, making themselves self-sustaining for their water needs. It's unlikely you will be allowed to dig a well in the suburbs because of the necessary permits and restrictions, but if you live in a small town or rural community and you don't have a well, check out the possibilities of installing one. Certainly there will be some initial costs, but it's worth the investment to have fresh water in a crisis situation. If you do have a well or if you install one, get a hand pump in addition to the electrical one. You can use the electrical one as long as possible, but if there is a blackout you will be able to pump the water by hand.

In addition to wells there are other sources of clean water: natural springs, creeks, and rainwater. You need to have this water tested to make sure it's safe before drinking it or using it in cooking. Even if it's not drinkable, the water can be used for irrigating, washing, and bathing. Anyone living in a wet climate has a perfect tool for gathering fresh drinking water: their home. Your roof and gutters serve as a rainwater collection device, so place a container at the end of a gutter's downspout and you'll capture all the water you need. Water troughs and barrels can be used for collecting rainwater. Be sure to purify this water before drinking it, especially if it has stood for any length of time.

In western and southern cities, many homes and apartment complexes have swimming pools. This could be a great water source for a number of families. Not only can this water be used for irrigating, washing, and bathing, but the water can be purified and made safe for drinking.

Purifying water is not a difficult procedure. Simply heat the water to a full rolling boil for at least 15 minutes. This process kills viruses and bacteria. You may need to strain the water to eliminate debris before you actually boil it. If you are high above sea level, add five minutes of boiling time for every thousand feet. The final element to purifying water is to add water purification tablets (available at sporting goods stores), iodine compounds, or simply a few drops of bleach. As a general rule, when in doubt, purify.

The Two- to Three-Day Plan

It just makes common sense to store additional water, so if you are planning for a short interruption of water service, purchase a five-gallon water jug and keep it stored in a closet in your home. It's good to know about options like existing water sources, alternative water sources, and purification procedures, but stockpiling water is simple and easy to do. You can also fill hard plastic containers and store them in your garage or closet.

Empty milk jugs work well for short periods of time, but the plastic leeches into the water when they are stored for a month or more. Use the "one gallon per person per day" rule and decide how much you need. For people living in hot, arid climates you may want to have more water set aside.

Three days without a bath might be a little uncomfortable for many people, but it is not an unreasonable period of time. Bathing on a daily basis was considered obsessive in America until the twentieth century, and your parents might very well have been raised in a "Saturday-night bath" culture, so don't feel you can't survive without your daily shower. (If you'll recall, one of the items we placed on the personal list was deodorant!)

Men don't need to shave every day, nor do women need to wash their hair every morning. If you have kept two quarts of water for drinking and two quarts for other activities like cooking, there will be plenty for brushing teeth and taking a sponge bath. *Remember, you don't know how long the emergency will last, and you don't want to waste a lot of water on the second day of a month-long crisis.*

What about the toilet? Even if you're planning just three days without water, do not use it. You won't be able to flush, and the smell will quickly become very unpleasant. You can keep a bucket of water close by to fill the tank each time, but that will quickly use up your water supply. Better to tape the toilet shut and use a portable chemical toilet. The solid waste will need to be buried, and the liquid waste can be poured onto the ground. If you don't have a portable toilet, use a bucket or small trash can and fill it with a plastic bag. We recommend two buckets, one for urine and one for excrement. If you have property, plan to bury the waste safely so the smell doesn't attract vermin.

The other option, and one still used in some areas of the country, is an outhouse. If you have a posthole digger, you can easily dig a hole for a usable outhouse. Of course, a shovel will work as well—you want the hole at least four feet deep, with loose dirt away from the top and flat bricks or blocks placed around the hole. After each use, toss in lime, which can be purchased from a building supply store. Make sure to keep this hole covered when not in use.

The One-Month Plan

For the One-Month Plan, an adult will need about 30 gallons of water. For a family of four, the needed amount is 120 gallons. However, one could halve that amount and be all right. Half a gallon of water per person is probably the least you want to have on hand, especially in hot or arid climates. If you have a limited supply of water and the crisis extends beyond three days, you may want to start cutting down your usage to a half gallon a day.

You will also want to start thinking about adding to your water supply. It's possible to purchase a large storage tank, but they are expensive and dangerously heavy. Instead, consider purchasing several five-gallon water jugs, or simply hanging on to your pop bottles and large jars.

If you store water in large tanks, secure the containers so they can't fall and hurt anyone. Even better, keep the water containers close to or on the floor of the storage area. Plastic containers are preferred because they are lighter in weight and won't break.

The water should be stored in a location which is both cool and dark. Heat and light are bad for water. If you fear it might freeze, leave room in the container so the water can expand without bursting it. A large freezer can also be used to store extra water—simply freeze it in blocks, then place the blocks in a portable cooler to keep perishables from spoiling. Once the water melts, you can then drink it or use it for washing.

Before storing water, make sure to clean the containers. Wash and rinse the bottle and the cap, but do not use detergent. The residue from detergent will be impossible to get completely out of the bottle and might contaminate the water. After rinsing, put at least four ounces of household bleach containing hypochlorite (ideally, 5.25 percent) into the container. Swirl the jug around to make sure the bleach covers all the surfaces, then pour out the bleach. Drain as much of it as you can, but do not rinse the container with water. You want the bleach to coat the surface with a thin film, then you can fill the bottle with cold, clean water for storage.

For drinking purposes, this water will last about six months if it is kept in a cool, dark place. If you are concerned about the safety of the water, simply add a few drops of chlorine bleach before drinking, shake it, and let it stand for 30 minutes. You may use tincture of iodine if you do not have bleach available. For one quart of clear water use two drops of bleach; for cloudy water use four drops. A gallon of clear water will require adding eight drops of bleach; 16 drops for cloudy water. If you are using a five-gallon container, use one half teaspoon for clear water, and one teaspoon for cloudy water.

Properly sealed, water can be kept outside, unless you are expecting a hard freeze. Water can also be held in a water storage trench. Dig a trench in the ground approximately 6 inches wide, 10 inches long and 36 inches deep. As long as the containers are sturdy and room has been provided at the top for expansion, the water may be frozen and it will not damage the supply. Remember, dark and cool are good for water, so a trench works very well. You can place about six one-gallon containers into the trench, then cover them with soil or sand to conceal the lids.

Of course, if you have stored enough water for a month, it won't be necessary to look for other sources. However, as the end of the month begins to approach, you may want to start searching for more water and rationing what you have. Realize that no one knows how long the emergency will last, so it makes sense to consider extending and apportioning your supplies as soon as the crisis begins. The emergency might last a month just because it takes that long to fix the power grid and get the system operating again. It's also possible billing problems could prevent you from getting your normal utility service for several months, particularly if you live in an outlying area. We suggest you keep hard copies of paid bills and check stubs so you can prove you don't owe 10,000 dollars on your water bill!

Make sure you reserve water for cooking, in addition to water for cleaning. In a three-day crisis there may not be much cooking, but in an emergency lasting a month or more you will have to be cooking. Water for cooking can be recycled for cleaning and watering living plants. Gray water—that is, used soapy water—can be strained and reused for washing again, or it can be poured onto your garden crops.

After three days, you will no doubt want to bathe. Don't take a bath—begin with sponge baths. When you do start taking baths, in a family, share the bathwater. Let one of the parents take a bath and then have one of the kids bathe in the same water, or have two kids bathe at the same time. The important thing is to *have a plan for rationing the water.* Five inches of water in a tub—about 20 gallons—is enough, so don't overfill. If there is no water being distributed, it means more than likely there is no electricity, so you will have to heat the water. This can be done outside over a fire pit, then carried inside to fill the tub. Find a big container to boil the water in, and make the fire pit large enough to hold the big pot.

Your portable chemical toilet or bucket system will work for up to a week, but after that amount of time, it's best to build an outhouse. Make sure the holes are deep and the toilet has a lid of some kind so the snow or rainwater doesn't run into it and cause overflow problems. Sanitation is very important during an emergency, and you want to make sure this part of your survival is handled correctly. Keep the lid on the toilet at all times when it's not in use. Bad sanitation spreads disease—make sure everyone in your family unit is aware of this. You will also have to deal with garbage and spoiled food. Bury this, and do not be tempted to put it onto a compost heap. It will attract rats, and with rats comes disease.

Another part of sanitation is to develop the habit of thoroughly washing your hands. Yes, you are rationing the water supply, but you need enough to keep clean, particularly those people who are preparing food. Use soap and hot water, and wash for at least 15 seconds—experienced outdoorsmen will tell you to sing the "Happy Birthday" song while washing, since it takes about the right amount of time. With a little planning, you can create a survival plan that provides your family with plenty of water for a month or more.

The One-Year Plan

For most people it's very difficult to imagine having no power or water for an entire year. Even in natural disasters, it rarely takes a full month to get some kind of water and power reestablished. Y2K is unlike other disasters because it affects so many different systems at the same time. Remember, even if one entire industry is Y2K compliant, its suppliers and vendors may not be. So if the banking industry is unable to collect payments from utility customers, it will definitely hurt the water companies. Technology has created many interdependent agencies, and it is this interdependence that will create headaches.

An emergency situation lasting a year without power and water sounds almost unthinkable. Rather than local outages or bill problems, it would almost necessarily be due to a mechanical shutdown due to a massive national power failure. If you believe the Y2K crisis will last as long as a year, you should also expect civil unrest especially in the cities. In that case, it's time for you to start considering moving away from the city. Expect derision from your friends and family members, since most people simply don't believe the Y2K problem could ever be this extreme.

The move itself will probably create much tension and stress in your family, but if you are going to make this transition from the city to the country, it is best to do it now. This requires advance planning. Don't wait until the crisis occurs, because you will have a far worse situation. Evacuating to the country in the middle of a national emergency will be at best very difficult. Traveling during a disaster is always dangerous. Evacuation means leaving your dwelling and most of your personal belongings behind. If you own your home in the city, you're going to have to decide what you plan to do with it. It's difficult enough to leave a rented apartment with a deposit, but can you really leave your largest financial investment behind?

Also, think through how and where you expect to find a place to live. You may have a lot of competition for property, since supply and demand will cause prices in the country to inflate. We can guarantee someone will be making a very good profit from the sales, and available land will be expensive. If you decide you must move to the country, we encourage you to take the time to make all the precautions we have mentioned. Stocking supplies for a year requires time and energy. Setting up a permanent outhouse, getting a garden started, and digging a well require an investment of time, space, and energy. Again, this kind of commitment will need a detailed plan.

The thought of Y2K lasting a year, at least in any significant way, is scary. But if you fear it is what the future will bring, you had best begin making plans now to take care of your family and loved ones.

YOUR Y2K PLANNING GUIDE

A 20-Point Family Water Checklist

1. Store one gallon of water per person per day for at least a three-day supply. Store more if you think the problem will persist. Use clean plastic bottles.
2. Be aware of existing water sources like the toilet tank and water heater.
3. If appropriate, have a well with a manual pump.
4. Consider other sources of clean water like springs and rainwater.
5. Know how to purify water—strain it, boil for 15 minutes, and add purification tablets.
6. Store water in a cool, dark, dry location.
7. Rinse containers with water and then rinse with chlorine bleach.
8. Leave room in the container for possible freezing and expansion.
9. Stored water lasts about six months.
10. Consider digging a storage trench to hold the family water supply.
11. Consider ways of adding to your water supply (for example, rainwater collection).
12. Know your comfort levels for bathing and talk to your family about this issue. Consider sponge-bathing as an alternative to a shower or bath.
13. Duct tape your toilet shut and use a portable chemical toilet or two-bucket system.
14. If the Y2K problem persists, consider building an outhouse.
15. Realize the importance of sanitation during a crisis. Keep all toilet lids closed, and be aware of potential problems with vermin and disease.
16. Reserve water for washing and cooking.
17. Always wash hands if preparing food.
18. Use gray water for plants.
19. Extend bathwater by using it for two or more people.
20. Bury sewage and garbage.

SEVEN

Safe and Warm

In an average year, 9000 to 10,000 Americans suffer from frostbite. But the year 2000 will not be average. If the heat is turned off, and with the threat to the power grid, the potential for suffering is greatly increased. How many people will suffer frostbite? How many people will simply freeze to death?

Most Americans don't know what it's like to be in an unheated dwelling in the middle of winter—we take indoor heating for granted. Fifty percent of our energy bill is spent on keeping us warm. How will you stay warm in January 2000 if your electricity goes off? Even if you heat your dwelling with gas or oil, the thermostat and fans are electric. For those people living in southern California, Florida, and southern Texas, losing indoor heating probably won't matter much, but it will matter a great deal to those in Minneapolis, Chicago, and New York City.

What's Ahead

- **Keeping Warm**
- **Heating Your Home**
- **A Heat Source**
- **The Two- to Three-Day Plan**
- **The One-Month Plan**
- **The One-Year Plan**
- **Your Y2K Planning Guide**

Keeping Warm

There are several things we can do that will make it easier to endure a cold winter and not depend on the utility companies. We can keep our bodies warm, insulate our homes, and use alternative heating sources that do not rely on electricity. Long underwear might conjure up images of cartoon hillbillies, but it's a practical and inexpensive way to keep warm. You want polyester, because it hugs the body and insulates better than other kinds of fabric. It's best if it has a turtle or crew neck, to lessen body heat escaping out the top of the underwear. Make sure the sleeves and pant legs are long enough to cover wrists and ankles. You also want a long-bodied top which tucks in below the waist. And you'll want bottoms that don't creep down the hips when you walk.

Dress in two or three layers so you can stay warm but add or remove clothing easily. Wear turtlenecked shirts under cotton shirts or vests, and a sweater over the entire outfit. Be sure wool sweaters and heavy sweatshirts are part of your winter wardrobe, and wear oversized corduroy or flannel shirts on top of sweatshirts or sweaters. Wool fingerless gloves will keep your hands warm without impeding finger movement, and heavy sports socks will keep your feet comfortable. You might even want to wear two pairs of socks if you plan to be outdoors for any length of time.

A hot water bottle can be placed between two layers of clothing for additional heat—it's a great way to keep warm while you're reading a book or sleeping. Have one hot water bottle for everyone in your family. The water can be gray water, since its only purpose is to provide heat, and you can use the hot water bottle to preheat the bed before sleeping in it. You might also want to try using simple hand warmers which run on lighter fluid and are sold in sporting-goods stores.

Down comforters will keep you warm in bed. Consider replacing cotton sheets with flannel ones, since they are warmer, and you might want to invest in some sleeping bags. They can be added to your bed like comforters, and you might find it necessary to have your entire family sleeping in one room near the heat source. Sleeping bags will be far easier to move around than beds, and are generally warmer and more comfortable than blankets and pillows on the floor. If several of you sleep in the same room, you can add to the heat by using candles, but be careful with fires and make sure someone is awake at all times to watch the flame.

If you are dealing with open fires of any sort, it will be to everyone's benefit to practice fire safety. Make sure everyone knows what to do in the event of a small fire, and have ABC fire extinguishers and a bucket of sand next to the wood stove or fireplace. If a small fire begins and you believe it is containable, evacuate children, the aged, and handicapped from the building, yell for help, and use sand or a chemical fire extinguisher to put out the fire. Of course you should use water hoses, but we don't know if the water power will be working. Follow carefully any written instructions on a fire extinguisher, and teach your kids to always spray back and forth at the base of the fire.

Use blankets in other rooms besides the bedroom. They'll be helpful for additional warmth during passive activities like reading, playing games, or knitting—you can even wear a blanket like a robe. Physical activity is another great way to maintain warmth, and is recommended if you are outdoors for extended periods of time. Be sure to exercise your legs, feet, and hands. If you must go outside, make sure you are wearing warm clothing and that you stay dry. You do not want to be both cold and wet, particularly if you aren't sure the hospitals are open!

Heating Your Home

Some very simple procedures can help you maintain heat in your dwelling. *Don't waste heat on vacant rooms and unused space.* Instead, keep doors closed to these areas. Don't heat the basement unless you're spending a lot of time there, and keep the dampers inside the heating ducts shut to keep heat out of unused rooms. Keep only the main rooms heated during the day, not the bedrooms. An hour or two before bedtime, you can open the bedroom doors. Keep the window drapes closed at night, and be sure to use drapes that fit tightly around the windows. Heavy, snug drapes will lessen the amount of cold air coming into your house. During sunny winter days, open the drapes and let the sunlight into your home—wintertime sun-light has a lot of heat.

If your dwelling has a fireplace chimney (and these days most fireplaces are more for decoration than actual heating), realize the chimney is your greatest source of heat loss. An open damper allows the loss of more heat than an open window because heat rises. Be certain to close the damper when not using your fireplace, and consider installing a glass door across the fireplace to further block heat from escaping.

A poorly insulated house can lose up to 50 percent of its heat. Usually utility companies offer inspections for free or at greatly reduced costs. Take advantage of these offers by gas and electric companies and invite them to inspect your house. They will check the house to discover where insulation is needed, and will offer advice on windows and doors. The United States Department of Energy recommends walls and floors of houses be insulated to values as high as R-19. (The R-value measures the resistance to heat flow—the higher the number, the greater the resistance.) According to those recommendations, ceilings in homes across the southern United States should be insulated to R-30. Homes in the midwestern states are recommended to have R-38, and homes in the north should have a rating of R-49.

If you live in a home built before 1970, check to see if the insulation in the attic and beneath floors meets the Department of Energy's recommended R-values by measuring the average depth of the insulation in your attic and floor. Contact your local lumber or hardware store with your figures, and ask for an estimate of the R-values. You can improve the heat efficiency of an older home yourself by adding insulation to the attic and beneath the floors. Lay insulation over the back of your attic door and weather-strip the edges, making sure the backing of insulation material is toward the heated area.

Don't forget your windows—the higher the R-value for windows, the more prepared you are. Most windows have a rating of R-2 or R-4, but you can get them as high as R-8. If you are thinking about replacing your current windows, consider

R-8 rated windows. They will be more expensive, but they are much more heat efficient. And use low-emissivity films, which can be applied to your existing windows to increase the R-values. Films insulate and upgrade your existing windows, reflecting heat back toward its source. In the winter the heat is reflected toward your furnace, and in the summer toward the sun.

Make sure to check your windows to see if they are tightly fitted, because loose-fitting windows will leak heated air five times faster than properly installed ones. There is an easy way to test them: Take a candle and move it around the perimeter of each window from the inside of the house on a windy day. If gusts of wind agitate the flame, the wind currents are leaking through the window and you need to caulk the frames. Caulking will plug the holes. For best results, caulk from inside the house. Although caulking on the outside keeps out moisture, it is less effective for retaining heat. You might also consider adding storm windows, which cut in half the amount of heat leakage through conventional windows. The cheapest do-it-yourself storm windows are made from polyethylene plastic and are installed from the inside with double-stick tape. While not terribly attractive, they are efficient and will help keep your home warm.

Check your outside doors and use weather stripping to seal gaps and leaks around the frames. If you are building a new house, make sure your outside doors are insulated, and even if you have an older home you might want to replace old doors with insulated ones. Install a door sweep along the bottom edge of the door, and staple ¾" diameter foam pipe insulation to the bottom of your garage door to cut down on heat loss through the garage. You can also wrap fiberglass insulation around the heating and air-conditioning ducts in the basement, attic, and crawl spaces. If there is less than 2 ½" of insulation around these ducts, simply wrap them with more insulation. There is no reason to strip off old insulation.

For apartment dwellers, consider where in the building you are located. The best place to be is on the middle floor, so that you get heat from both above and below. Although it will probably be at your own expense, consider simple, low-cost additions like plastic storm windows, heavy drapes, and door sweeps. One easy alternative to a door sweep is to place a rolled-up rug at the bottom of your door.

A Heat Source

Due to power failures, your electric, gas, and oil heat are unlikely to work during the Y2K crisis. A pellet stove is not an alternative heating source, since it relies on electricity. You could get your own portable electric generator, but realize you will need gas fuel for it, which requires very careful storage. For city dwellers a generator is more of a liability than a solution.

The most likely alternative fuel is wood, the world's most commonly used source of energy. *If you currently have a fireplace, you will want to think about converting it to a wood-burning stove or installing an insert.* The downside to wood fuel is the need for a large, dry storage area and the rising expense of buying wood. Due to the fact it is the most popular alternative to conventional heating sources, there will doubtless be a huge demand for the product, and you can expect prices to begin increasing in the fall of 1999.

If you are going to use wood, the best type is hardwood from deciduous trees. These trees—like oak, maple, beech, ash, and locust—lose their leaves in the autumn and offer a much hotter-burning fuel than evergreen softwoods like spruce, pine, and fir. Softwoods burn less efficiently, giving you less heat per cord, and create creosote—the smelly, oily liquid that lines chimneys and causes most chimney fires. It can be removed if you have the correct cleaning tools, but it's a dirty, messy job and must be done frequently.

Storing a quantity of hardwood in a secure location like your garage or shed will provide you with heat during the cold days of January 2000.

The Two- to Three-Day Plan

To prepare for a two- or three-day emergency, begin by checking the current heating efficiency of your home. Check all your insulation and improve it if needed. Practice heat conservation by closing unused rooms, turning down the heat when leaving the house, and employing the other tactics mentioned earlier. *You want heat-saving strategies to become an ingrained habit for you and everyone in your family.* Do not put this off. Even if the Y2K crisis is short, you will benefit by seeing your heating bill reduced.

Check your emergency kit and be certain you have stored enough blankets, sleeping bags, winter clothing, rain gear, candles, and hot water bottles. You'll want to consider getting a camp stove, if you don't have one. Use this for cooking, but do not depend upon this or other devices that burn gas or kerosene to be your heat source. Of course, you should never use your charcoal grill to heat your dwelling. All of these create carbon monoxide when burning, so you will need to use them in well-ventilated areas, and only for short periods of time. In addition to the possibility of carbon monoxide poisoning is the danger of fire. Every winter, lethal fires are started by people trying to gain additional heating by using kerosene and gas-burning appliances. Practice fire safety and be extremely careful using these items around your home.

If you live in an area of the United States where the winters do not get extremely cold, you are probably going to endure a two- or three-day crisis reasonably well. Perhaps you won't be as comfortable as you would like, but you will be able to survive the hardships without much misery. Extra blankets and warm clothing might be just enough to get you through the emergency. However, give special attention to infants, the elderly, and the sick. They often need more heat to feel comfortable.

If you live in a part of the country where it gets intensely cold, consider making a trip to a warmer location. While we wouldn't advise traveling on December 31 or January 1, we would suggest a warmer climate as a pleasant alternative. If this is a possibility, start planning your trip now. Make sure you have somewhere to stay—friends and family are best. If Y2K hits really hard, you won't want to be in a hotel in a large urban area or in a Third World country. You want to be able to extend your stay if you need to, and this will be easier to do with people who care about you. It is also wise to know your hosts' feelings about Y2K. You all should be of the same mind-set. We doubt you'll want to stay with people who are not prepared for an emergency. After all, this trip is predicated on the concept of a Y2K scenario.

If you plan to drive to a temporary refuge, make sure you have a small emergency survival kit in the car as a backup. You'll want warm clothes, sleeping bags, flashlights, and a small amount of food and water. Candles are also handy to have, since one lit candle can keep the inside of a car above freezing level. Remember to keep some ventilation by cracking open a window.

Again, most fireplaces aren't terribly efficient, but for a two- or three-day emergency situation it doesn't really matter. If you have a fireplace or a wood stove, make sure you have enough wood to burn 12 hours a day for three days. You'll probably want to start stockpiling now, while it's still cheap. The longer you wait to buy wood, the more expensive it will become. It takes six months to cure wood and make it burnable, and at least a month to dry out wet wood, so make sure you have plenty stored under a tarp or in another covered area for at least a month before you need it.

The One-Month Plan

A month without heat in the dead of winter, especially in a cold part of the world, would be at best a very unpleasant experience—and at worst it could be lethal. If you have planned for a month-long emergency or longer you will probably be all right. The better prepared you are for a long emergency, the better you will fare. *If you expect the crisis to last a month, plan for it.* Have plenty of warm clothes, blankets, and other items mentioned throughout this chapter, and consider getting a wood stove for heating and cooking.

Many wood stoves are designed only for heating, so if you're considering buying one, make sure you select one that will allow you to cook. Old wood cooking stoves can sometimes be found in classified ads and at garage sales. If you buy a used one, be certain it is clean, workable and meets all legal code requirements. Remember to choose heating and cooking stoves that do not need electricity to blow or circulate heat, and look for high-efficiency wood-burning stoves that give out the maximum amount of heat. Preferably you want to be able to stoke it up, shut the damper, and not need to reload it for up to eight hours. If you currently have only a fireplace, you can probably convert it to a wood-burning stove. A fireplace simply isn't efficient enough to rely on for a full month, especially in a cold location.

If wood is your fuel, make sure you have plenty safely stored. A month's supply—at least two cords—will take up a lot of space. And at least some of the storage space has to be covered so the wood is kept dry.

The other major alternative is to leave your home for a month and stay with family or friends in a warmer climate. This option was discussed in the two- to three-day section above, so ask yourself: Are the people you will be living with prepared for additional visitors and have enough foodstuffs to supply everyone for a full month? Also consider what it means to be gone from your home for a month in the middle of a national emergency. If your home is in a small, safe community, you will probably fare better than if your home is located in the middle of a large city.

The One-Year Plan

We will assume that if you believe the crisis could last a year, you are already making plans to move to a place in the country. Farming will be necessary for survival in a long-term emergency, so you should plan to be raising your own food supply. It can be as simple as a large vegetable garden, or as elaborate as a ranch.

Look for an area to live which is at least 100 miles from cities with a population of 100,000 or more. Find land with rich, fertile soil, a good water source like a spring, and plenty of timber. The timber might be used for building, but it will probably be used for fuel. The location is better if it's sheltered from wind by trees or hills. You do not want a site that has a lot of wind, because it will have an impact on the warmth of your home. Remember: *Farm life is very affected by the natural elements.*

The amount of land you will need depends upon the number of people you are going to support and what you intend to raise. For a "truck farm," growing only vegetables, the size of the land needed is roughly two acres for each person. If you plan on having chickens, you will need to add another acre. Cows require a great deal of land, so this kind of commitment is beyond the scope of most people. If you want a source for milk, consider goats, which only require three to five acres.

If you build a new home, find land with a southward-facing slope and construct the house facing south with most of the windows on the south side. This will allow you to take advantage of the sun's southerly position in winter and help create additional warmth. The sun is overhead in the summer and will not shine in your southern windows. Avoid low areas because of flooding. If you can, build the house at least 60 feet downhill from a spring. This will give you adequate water pressure for your home without needing to pump. Additionally, build the house out of sight from the road for security reasons, and don't build downwind of the barn if you have animals!

Even if you have a site with trees, you might consider getting a generator. While we think a generator is impractical for most urban living, it's a wise investment for rural life. You will want to stock enough fuel to last two years. Keep the fuel away from the living quarters and away from children. If you do decide to purchase a generator, connect it to at least one household circuit for appliances, such as a refrigerator or battery chargers. Invest in a kerosene freezer if you have enough money to do so.

Your home will need a wood stove that can serve as the main heat source. Ideally, you will have your own timber, so you won't need to buy it, but you will need to replace the trees you use. You will also need tools to get firewood. Firewood requires a lot of work: cutting, splitting, stacking, and curing can quickly wear a man out. It's best to cut up dead trees and save the living ones. If you need to cut down a live tree, realize it will take about a year before the wood can be burned. The best time to split wood is in the winter, since the cold makes the wood more brittle and easier to cut. Keep cutting tools like an ax in a reasonably warm area, otherwise the blades will get brittle and chip. And keep your wood dry for at least a month before burning it. Wet wood is difficult to burn and produces less heat. In addition to the firewood, you will need kindling to start the fire—you can use bark, corn cobs, small dried branches, and even pine cones. The best practice is to keep your fire going from the end of the fall to the beginning of spring, so you won't need to start a new fire every day.

You might also want to check out other sources of power, including solar and wind generators. Realize they are expensive to set up, but inexpensive to maintain. If Y2K does last a year, you will also want to know how to keep cool during the summer. Air-conditioning won't be available, so during hot periods open the doors and windows at night to let in the cool air. In the morning, shut down the house, closing everything and sealing in the cool air. Cook outdoors in the summertime to eliminate cooking heat in your house, and use devices like awnings to shade the house and keep it cool.

YOUR Y2K PLANNING GUIDE

20 Things Your Family Can Do to Stay Warm

1. Wear long polyester underwear.
2. Have winter clothes and dress in layers.
3. Use hot water bottles to add to personal warmth.
4. Use down comforters and extra sleeping bags.
5. Have several people sleep in the same room.
6. Use candles for heat, but be careful with open flames.
7. Know fire safety and have fire extinguishers and buckets of sand ready.
8. Use physical exercise to keep warm.
9. Don't waste heat on vacant rooms and unused space.
10. Use window drapes to keep heat in and cool air out. Close drapes at night; open them during sunny days.
11. Be certain to close the damper when not using your fireplace. Consider installing a glass door across the fireplace to further block heat from escaping.
12. Make sure your house is properly insulated. Find out what R-values are required where you live and make sure your insulation is at least that high.
13. Check windows for R-value ratings, make sure the windows are tightly fitted, and use low-e films on windows to reflect heat.
14. Consider adding storm windows.
15. Add weather stripping and sweeps to doors if needed.
16. Apartment dwellers should live on a floor between upper and lower floors.
17. Consider converting your fireplace to a wood-burning stove.
18. Know how to get firewood and have all the proper tools. Stockpile hardwood now while it is still inexpensive.
19. If where you live gets intensely cold in the winter, consider making a trip to a warmer location. Plan a trip now to stay with like-minded Y2K people, and donate your portion to the stockpile.
20. If you are going to move to the country, know what kind of land you want and how much you will need. Be prepared for a major lifestyle change.

EIGHT

Light and Power

Americans are electricity junkies. The average American home has more than 100 items which require electricity. Certainly some of these things are vital to the safety and efficiency of our home, but we take electricity for granted. Most of us don't think much about electricity until the power goes out, but *then* we realize the significance of its loss.

On July 3, 1996, there was a mega-power outage throughout eight western states. It affected a broad range of homes, from Oregon to Nevada and two Canadian provinces—the electrical supply for nearly two million people was impaired. Air traffic controllers and hospitals were compelled to use emergency generators. Traffic lights shut off. Elevators stopped. Banks closed. Refrigerators, air-conditioners, and freezers quit running on a day in which the heat was as high as 100 degrees in some cities. The repercussions were substantial, though the random outages didn't last long—in most cases, less than two hours. Consider the ramifications of a day's loss, a week's, or a month's. How would your life be changed if you couldn't flick a switch and have the lights come on?

What's Ahead

- **Going Black**
- **Making Changes**
- **Light and Dark**
- **The Two- to Three-Day Plan**
- **The One-Month Plan**
- **The One-Year Plan**
- **Your Y2K Planning Guide**

We've already discussed the possible fallout when heat, water, and food are dependent upon electrical power. But the loss of light and power create other problems, which can affect us emotionally. Psychologists recognize that the dreary gray light of winter can cause mental depression. Darkness can stimulate irrational fear. What could happen when you turn out the lights on 200 million people?

Going Black

Is it really possible that many people will be involved? The biggest concern of a potential national electrical failure is the grid phenomenon. Since America's electrical power consists of a grid of power stations tightly interconnected, a blackout in one place can easily trigger another blackout in another place. It's believed only three power stations were knocked out in the incident of 1996, yet the result was felt across the country. So keep in mind that even if your local utility is Y2K compliant, other power companies could cause it to lock up. Little failures in one spot can be transferred in seconds across states, causing big failures in several cities at the same time. In fact, *the main worry is not with large utilities, but with smaller ones which are still on the grid.*

A super-blackout is likely to cause permanent damage to network equipment such as high-voltage breakers, transformers, and generation plants. If this were to happen, it would render them unavailable for restoring power. What this means is a "rolling blackout," which occurs so quickly utilities can't get off the grid fast enough to stop from being shut down. If too many power plants go down simultaneously, there may not be enough power anywhere else in the system to get the dormant plants activated again. The United States has never witnessed a far-flung, multiregional blackout, so no one can predict the outcome.

To complicate matters, the Y2K problem will be crossing national boundaries. If the power goes out in Japan, Western countries will know it hours ahead of time. But will they be able to do anything to prevent it happening here? If the power goes out in the United States, the impact on the world is unimaginable.

Making Changes

So what do we do? We need to begin planning for a major electric blackout. One area of that plan will involve material supplies and alternative energy systems. Another part of the plan involves our emotional and psychological preparation. Examine your current reliance on electric power and light. *Start cutting back and simplifying your life for the purpose of learning to live with less.* Better to adjust to this idea now, when you have the option of choosing to live this way, than when you are forced to make changes for which you are unprepared. If you are accustomed to living without as much electricity, you won't be quite as upset when it is gone.

You might start by turning off the television and the VCR, leaving them off for an entire day. For some people, living without TV is a pleasure and not a punishment. In fact, many families have made the decision in recent years to shut off the TV or get rid of it entirely, since they were tired of the destructive force they saw it becoming in their lives. For others the adjustment will be hard. "But the kids won't know what to do with themselves!" True, they might be surprised by the action, but if you turn it into a game, they'll have an easier time adjusting to the sacrifice. "Let's see how long we can go without the TV," you suggest. "The person who lasts the longest will get a prize."

What happens when the television goes dark? It's hard to imagine, but there was a time before television existed. In those nearly forgotten days, people read, played games, and talked to one another. They would gather around the piano and sing. We recommend you try the "no-TV challenge" and see how you and your family do. The key to success is making it fun. Then on another day, try giving up something else. Make these initial forfeitures simple—choose things that are not necessities. Try living a weekend without using a toaster, the coffee-maker, or the dishwasher. Those things are certainly convenient, but they are not necessary to your survival.

On another night, use candlelight only. Most of us have experienced a blackout caused by a storm, and we have survived the situation, perhaps even enjoyed it. A little adversity can be a bonding experience. Since the "lights out" challenge is not perceived as a crisis, the anxiety level will be low. After you have tried giving up a number of different items for small amounts of time, take a bigger step. Perhaps you could restrict television to only a few nights a week, use the coffeemaker only on Sunday mornings, or turn on the dishwasher only if more than five people have a meal at one time.

Examine your use of lights: Do you have a light on in an unoccupied room? Do you use a higher-powered lamp instead of a low-wattage night-light? Does the porch light stay on all night? Is the TV on all the time, even when you aren't in the room? Perhaps you already practice electric conservation. If you don't, begin doing so now. Use only enough light to see well. We obviously don't want you hurting your vision or causing accidents, but you might discover you need a lot less light than you thought.

Over a period of time, perhaps two or three months, you can cut down on more and more appliances for greater lengths of time. You might see your electrical bill decrease, and you will certainly find you don't rely on as many things as you once did. That's a good lesson to learn, even if Y2K fizzles out and doesn't cause the anticipated troubles. Perhaps one positive thing about the threat of Y2K is the need for each of us to reexamine our lives and our dependencies. It's possible we've all become a little too comfortable, a little too fat, and a bit too wasteful. Each year Americans spend two billion dollars on purposeless outdoor light that shines upward and accomplishes nothing. It shouldn't take much "sacrifice" to give up our porch lights and flag lamps!

Light and Dark

The psychological adjustment will probably be more trying than stockpiling supplies and working out alternative energy solutions. Getting materials together will require time, money, and space, but it's a defined task, unlike attempting to sort out your thoughts and feelings about living with less. Learning to change the way we live is a tougher problem, with much richer results.

Finding an alternative to standard electricity poses a problem. Many people are buying electric generators. In fact, so many people are doing this that there is already beginning to be a shortage of generators. The president of China Diesel Imports, the largest United States distributor of diesel generators, recently noted that orders were up more than 1000 percent, and that the most popular models were running out fast. Originally, China Diesel Imports supplied country customers living outside the reach of electric utilities, but now most of the customers are people concerned about the potential outcome of Y2K. The company currently has both of the world's largest generator manufacturers working at near capacity just to satisfy U.S. demand.

For an average-size home with a family of four, the size of the generator needed would be from 3500-5000 watts. But even with a large generator, not all appliances will run. For example, refrigerators and freezers require much more power. And high-tech or computer-controlled items might have problems unless they have been carefully adjusted to your home wiring. Of course, basic things like small appliances and lights won't have any trouble. At the end of 1998, the average cost for a 3500-watt generator was about 1800 dollars, and a 5000-watt generator sold for about 2300 dollars. On top of that, to be safe, you will need a transfer switch which cuts off the electrical connection to the power company. This means an additional 50 dollars to 200 dollars in costs. Not only that, with the demand being high, you can expect the costs to increase substantially as the supply lessens and the demand increases. And that only pays for the generator itself—you also have to buy fuel!

In order to run your generator, you need diesel or unleaded gas, though some generators can be converted to propane. (This conversion is expensive and not usually recommended by dealers.) To run your generator for six to eight hours, the amount of gas needed is roughly five gallons, or about seven dollars in American money. In a week you would use 35 gallons of gas. To run a generator for a full 24 hours, you would need up to 20 gallons of gas, costing roughly 30 dollars a day.

The problem with that is the potential for gas shortages. Currently, you can go to the gas station whenever you want and buy gas. There hasn't been a severe gas shortage in the United States since the late 1970s. But a major electric outage would significantly affect drilling, refinement, and transportation, which means there's a high probability the gas station won't have gas when you need it. Even if distribution is not hindered, there's a very good possibility that crowds of people will be demanding gas. If that happens, the supply won't last long and prices will skyrocket. What good is having a generator if you can't get gas to run it?

This means you would need to start stockpiling gas—a practice we discourage, since gas is potentially dangerous and the storage needs much more attention than most other supplies. Where will you keep 30 gallons of gas? Certainly you'll want to store it safely, but if you're using candles and oil lamps, you're living with open flame—a recipe for disaster. Some people will argue storing gas is not that big a deal, since most of us have at least one car, and usually there are 5 to 15 gallons in it. But we contend that's not the same as three separate five-gallon containers kept in a basement. A car is one thing—three cans of gas increase the chances for accidents, simply because you have increased the number of items. If you plan on storing gas, you'll need to make everyone in your family aware of the potential danger. And have plenty of fire extinguishers and sand buckets for emergencies. If the power isn't working, you may not be able to contact your local fire department.

The choice to have a portable generator is obviously a personal one, but realize it's expensive, limited in use, and possibly dangerous. How badly do you need a generator? There is a valid argument that a business might need one, but a home probably doesn't. *We believe that the average home doesn't need much electricity.* There are many small conveniences that run on batteries, including radios and portable televisions. A wood stove will give you heat and allow you to cook. And candles, flashlights, and a fireplace will offer your family the light you need. Besides, the money you save on the generator could more wisely be spent on food, warm clothing, a good propane stove, and a source of heat. Perhaps our standard of living has reached the point where we crave electricity more than we need it.

The Two- to Three-Day Plan

Three days without electricity shouldn't be much of a hardship—many of us give it up for at least that long when we go on a camping trip. As long as you have provided for heat, cooking, and light, you should be fine. If you are using a generator, you will want enough gasoline for three days—about 15 gallons. That's enough for 18-24 hours of use.

For light sources, you'll want candles and flashlights, which means you'll also need to stock up on matches, lighters, and batteries. Make sure you have long-lasting batteries and plenty of them, as well as having different sizes. In addition to flashlights and transistor radios, know which of your important belongings run on batteries, and be certain to have enough of the appropriate sizes. Discount stores often sell large quantities of batteries at low costs. If the electricity is out, you will not be able to recharge your rechargeable batteries, so it's better to rely on long-lasting ones. Check the expiration date on the packaging before purchasing.

Two or three candles per room should be enough light. Naturally, candlelight is not strong enough to read by, but it will be good for plenty of other activities. The size of the candle will determine the length of time it will burn. Try to find long-burning candles that last four to six hours. You may not want to have the candles burning constantly, so you can put them out until you need them. For three days, a supply of about two dozen long-lasting candles should be plenty. Just make sure you have matches or lighters to get them going. Matches are easier, since they require fewer elements. A lighter requires fluid and a flint, which means you will need to have those additional things, just in case. The only requirement matches have are a striking surface and dry conditions. A disposable cigarette lighter can also come in handy.

For flashlights, you'll want to have additional bulbs and batteries. Use flashlights which put out a good, strong light. Several flashlights scattered throughout your home will make life a little easier. When the lights are not in use, turn them off. You do not want to waste them.

A kerosene lantern would be nice, but is not really necessary for a three day emergency. If you intend on using kerosene lamps, you will need to store your kerosene safely. Another possibility is to use oil lamps. These give out a bright light and are very simple to operate, but make sure you store plenty of oil. Due to the reliance on liquid fuel and their fragility—most lamps are made out of glass—you'll also want to talk with your kids about handling them carefully.

You might also consider getting some emergency light sticks. The light sticks are operated by what is known as "cold" light. That light doesn't generate heat enough for us to feel, but it does put out plenty of light (about the same amount as a single candle), and it lasts about six to eight hours. They are extremely safe, since they do not use fire. In fact, the only downside is that once they are turned on, they cannot be turned off. A light stick can only be used once. However, a two-bedroom house might only require two or three light sticks at a time to give sufficient light throughout the occupied areas. The light color is usually green, but you can find them in red and blue as well. It's not a good light to read by, but it will certainly illuminate an area enough to see what is happening. For a three-day emergency, you might store about a dozen light sticks, in addition to at least that many candles.

Another possible source, but not as well-known, is the use of hand-powered and solar-powered flashlights. Survivalist stores sell these, and the price range is typically between 30 dollars and 100 dollars, depending on the type of light. Some can be recharged by merely leaving them in the sunlight. The bodies of such lights are often quite sturdy because they are built to be used in emergency situations. The amount of light will last about three hours at a time before needing to be recharged. Some of these flashlights combine solar and battery power, which will extend the amount of running time. Other solar-powered lights available provide fluorescent light for up to four hours and use a combination of solar panel, standard batteries, and a 110-volt AC/DC adapter. Survivalist stores also sell wind-up lanterns. These are crank-operated and will provide about three minutes of light for every 30 seconds of winding time. Repeated winding cycles (60 turns each) while the light is turned off will charge the battery to higher levels. The light can be stored indefinitely with the spring fully wound up, allowing for instant light when needed, even if the battery is fully discharged.

Be aware that your location will determine the amount of light you need. The further north, the longer night lasts. Winter weather conditions also involve a lot of cloud cover, so even during the day, it's not often very bright. Factor the length of your daylight into the amount of supplies you will want to have. Someone living in Miami will need fewer supplies for light than someone living in Juneau.

Since we are using candles and perhaps kerosene or oil lamps, we need to think about fire safety. Again, make sure you have several working fire extinguishers and some sand buckets. Don't waste precious water, although you could save gray water to use for fire safety purposes. The buckets can be old coffee cans or other recycled containers. Baking soda can also be used as an alternative—it's nonflammable and produces carbon dioxide to smother the fire. Know where the buckets and extinguishers are, and keep them near your heating and cooking source.

The psychological impact of a two- or three-day emergency should not be great. In a few days there will probably be some anxiety about the length of the emergency and fears about the extent of the damage caused by Y2K. Having a radio will help keep you informed. Knowing what's likely to happen is far less fear-provoking than not knowing.

Battery-operated transistor radios have been in existence since the late 1950s. Make sure you have one and have enough batteries for it to last. Survivalist stores sell radios that do not rely on external electrical or battery power. There are radios that are powered by a textured carbon steel spring and energized by hand cranks. Typically, 30 seconds of winding creates enough energy for approximately 30 minutes of listening time. Some units can also be powered by a small solar panel and feature both AM and FM bands. Other radios available use a combination of power sources, including a hand-crank generator, built-in solar panel, and "AA" batteries. They provide longer play time, usually about an hour for two minutes of winding. Crystal radios offer another possibility. Crystal radio kits sell for less than 10 dollars and have a long life expectancy. However, they only receive AM stations.

Having heat, light, and information will help to improve your emotional state. Sitting in a cold, dark room, cut off from the world, is not where you want to be.

The One-Month Plan

The psychological impact of a month-long disaster is far greater than the emotional stress of a short-term emergency. Heat and light are very important to good mental health and awareness. A crisis of this length will require you to be mentally alert. If you are constantly fatigued from the cold and hunger and depressed from lack of light, your chances of survival are lessened.

Certainly a month-long calamity will require many more supplies than a three-day one. For a longer-lasting crisis, a portable generator would be a great thing to have. Rationing the use of the generator would be a key to using it effectively. The less it's operating on a daily basis, the longer it will function and the longer you will be able to stretch your supply of fuel. In order to err in your favor, assume five gallons of gas per day. For a 30-day crisis you would need to stock 150 gallons of gas. With careful rationing, you might be able to cut that in half. It's still a potential danger, so remember that the less gas you have in storage, the less chance for accidental fires.

A fire is something you really want to avoid even in the best of times, but in a crisis condition when the phones may not work and the standard emergency services may not be available, it's something no one wants to face. Make sure you have enough extinguishers available and that you practice fire safety as a family.

To prepare for a month-long crisis, have enough extra batteries and bulbs for all of your flashlights and other items like clocks and radios. Stock up on candles—one to two *gross* should be enough to last a month. Candles kept in the cold will burn longer than candles kept in room temperature, so you might want to put your candles outdoors for several hours prior to using them. Always remember to ration your supplies so you can extend their life span.

Kerosene and oil lamps will definitely be a plus if the lights are out for as long as 30-days. Plan to have enough fuel for the lamps to last a month. Kerosene lamps provide strong enough light to read by, though you may want to invest in one of the hand-operated or solar-powered lights mentioned earlier. We also strongly recommend you have at least one radio. Being without communication for three days is OK, but not for a month. You'll want to know what is going on around the rest of the world. The information could be necessary for you and your family's survival. Again, you can apportion the listening time so you make the batteries last longer. You might want to purchase a hand-operated, solar-powered, or crystal radio as a backup precaution.

The One-Year Plan

If you have committed to the concept of a year-long emergency, then you probably have bought an 8000-watt generator and have plenty of gas to operate it. Some people have converted their generators from unleaded gas to propane for storage convenience. Again, be aware of fire safety and make sure the gas is properly stored. Careful planning and rationing will extend the life of your generator. Don't waste the generator on small items like lights and radios. You will also want to know how to repair the generator if needed, and you will want to have the necessary parts to do so. Some people have chosen to invest in more than one generator, or to have a spare-parts kit on hand.

In a year's time, constant use will burn out a lot of batteries, so plan to have enough stocked to last a year. You might want to examine alternative sources like solar-powered or hand-powered lights and radios. A crystal radio will last for years, but as noted earlier, it only gets AM stations. If you are located far away from a large city, you will probably need to get an antenna for it.

The amount of candles needed to last a year is staggering, so much so that we suggest you consider getting enough supplies to make your own candles. If you have beehives, you have a source for beeswax candles. In addition to the wax, all you will need is string to act as a wick. The beeswax can be pressed and rolled into a candlestick.

For outdoor use you might want to consider creosote torches. You will probably limit your outdoor activity in the winter, but once spring begins you may find you want to be outside at night. Torches are an inexpensive way of accomplishing this. Outdoor fire pits will also create light outdoors. During the summer months you might want to do at least some of your cooking outside, even if you have an electric generator.

Don't overlook the use of kerosene and oil lamps. This will require a stockpiling of fuel, but the light is bright and strong enough to warrant the storage space. And by all means, don't underrate the psychological advantage of good lighting. Even primitive humanity understood that firelight gave them protection.

YOUR Y2K PLANNING GUIDE

15 Steps to Preparing for Light

1. Recognize the possibility of a mega-blackout and examine your current reliance on electric power and light.
2. Start simplifying your lifestyle. Practice giving up certain appliances and establish a "no-TV challenge" as a fun exercise.
3. Begin using more candles and less electrical lighting.
4. If you want an electric generator, buy one soon. They will be less expensive the sooner you buy. Understand the limitations of your generator—not all appliances will run on it.
5. Plan on having replacement parts and tools needed to fix the generator.
6. Plan on storing gas for the generator—roughly five gallons a day.
7. Practice fire safety and have plenty of fire extinguishers and sand buckets. Know that baking soda is also a good extinguisher.
8. Stock up on candles (about six per day). Candles stored in the cold burn longer. Also stockpile matches.
9. Stock up on long-lasting batteries and flashlight bulbs.
10. Consider kerosene and oil lamps. Don't forget fuel.
11. Light sticks do not put out any heat and last several hours, but they cannot be turned on and off. Plan to buy several.
12. Check out solar-powered lights and radios, as well as hand-powered lights and radios.
13. Build a crystal radio.
14. Use creosote torches in warmer weather and climates.
15. Don't forget the importance of rationing your energy and light resources.

PART THREE

▼

SOLVING PROBLEMS

NINE

Medical Questions

The impact of Y2K on medical service will severely affect the sick, the elderly, the handicapped, and infants. Because poor people rely on government help, they will feel the impact of reduced medical services more than the rich. With the exception of medical emergencies, mature healthy people will not be as concerned about limited medical aid.

The first thing you must consider is the necessity of your health and your family's health. Right now, do you know how healthy you are? If you or anyone in your family hasn't had a medical checkup in over a year, get one as soon as possible. This should also apply to dental examinations—dental emergencies can be lethal. If you have health problems, what do you need to do to take care of them? If you do have special medical needs, what alternatives do you have if you can't get immediate attention? What supplies do you need, and can they be stored for emergency use if necessary? The answers to these questions will vary from individual to individual and will determine what you will need to do to be ready for a crisis.

What's Ahead

- **Hospitals and Y2K**

- **First-Aid Supplies**

- **Treating Burns**

- **Winter Injuries**

- **Coughs, Colds, and Allergies**

- **Tummy Trouble**

- **The Two- to Three-Day Plan**

- **The One-Month Plan**

- **The One-Year Plan**

- **Your Y2K Planning Guide**

Your family should also consider the importance of wellness and prevention. Start working on improving your health. If you need to go on a diet, stop smoking, moderate your sugar or alcohol use, and exercise more, *begin now*. The last thing you want is to get sick during an emergency situation.

Hospitals and Y2K

It might be a very good idea to not schedule any major surgery the first several days of January 2000. Even though most hospitals have backup generators and are the first priority with utility companies, there could still be potential problems caused by power failures and the fact that *nearly all advanced hospital medical equipment depends on computers*. Certainly not all computer-based equipment is date-sensitive, but much is. The medical equipment most likely to be affected by Y2K includes pacemakers, heart defibrillators, intensive-care monitors, infusion pumps in intravenous drips, chemotherapy and radiation equipment, MRIs, CAT and PET scans, dialysis, radiology and other diagnostic systems, and many of the advanced tools in the laboratory.

Another area of concern is hospital administration, billing, and insurance programs. At the close of 1998, the Health and Human Service's Health Care Financing Administration (HCFA), which manages the Medicare program, had over 100 mission-critical systems of which only seven are currently Y2K compliant. If HCFA's systems are not Y2K compliant in time, then the collapse of the Medicare system is very likely. People who are dependent upon Medicare will be in trouble. Will your doctors accept Medicare patients if they know they won't be paid until 2001?

In addition to avoiding disease and sickness, you want to talk with your family about avoiding injury. You and your kids need to discuss basic safety practices for preventing burns and frostbite, tending to cuts, and dealing with falls and other injuries.

What areas of your survival life are the most accident-prone? Cooking offers a range of potential accidents: burning, cutting, and poisoning. In preparing a meal with your family, you want to practice commonsense procedures. First, make sure everyone washes their hands thoroughly. Second, examine your food stores and make sure they are safe and not spoiled. Third, check to be certain the water you use for cooking is not contaminated. Fourth, check the utensils you are working with and make sure they are clean. Fifth, be very careful when cutting, chopping, or grating food, and talk to your children about using hot pads and kitchen mitts for moving hot pots and pans on camp stoves or wood stoves. Remind everyone to be aware of sleeves and loose threads when near cooking fires, and keep small children and pets out of the kitchen.

Sixth, make sure the source you are using for heat is safe and doesn't produce carbon monoxide. Practice fire safety—don't leave burning candles and fires unattended. Make sure everyone knows how to use a fire extinguisher, and check to see that all extinguishers are working. Seventh, during the cold winter months, limit outdoor activity. Tell your family if they must go outside for extended periods, to keep warm and dry. When outdoors, be wary of stray animals. And above all, know where your children are and what they are doing.

Preventive measures such as these will help limit the number of injuries and illnesses. We know you can't prevent everything, and there is always the possibility of accidents, but a plan for safety and a thorough discussion of health concerns will help everyone be better prepared.

First-Aid Supplies

We suggest you purchase and store medical and first-aid supplies. The foundation of your medical supply should be a good first-aid guide. Assume you will not be able to contact a physician, except in life-threatening circumstances, and you won't be able to phone for an ambulance if the telephone isn't working (it's also possible the ambulance will either not work or be without gas, so we would give up the notion of relying on many emergency services). It's very likely that most hospitals will be overwhelmed and understaffed during Y2K, so *you may not be able to get any attention at all, even if your condition is life-threatening.*

Therefore, you are going to want to make sure your home has a well-stocked first-aid kit. You'll want to have adhesive-strip bandages in various sizes. These, along with Band-Aids, can be used for all sorts of minor injuries. For larger injuries you'll want gauze pads, possibly even sanitary napkins for use as a pressure dressing. You'll also need adhesive tape, hypoallergenic tape, triangular bandages, waterproof tape, roller gauze, elastic bandages, and nonadhering dressing.

Rubbing alcohol, hydrogen peroxide, antibiotic ointment, calamine lotion, and hydrocortisone cream are useful for various external conditions ranging from insect bites to poison ivy to cuts. Items such as chemical ice packs, chemical hot packs, cotton balls, cotton swabs, disposable latex gloves, ice bags, thermometers (both oral and rectal), tongue depressors, tweezers, safety pins, salt, scissors, soap, insect repellent, insect-sting swabs, household ammonia, a space blanket, splints, a face mask for CPR, a hot water bottle, matches, needles, and oil of cloves can be used to treat a number of conditions.

For internal trouble you'll want to have antacid, baking soda, decongestant tablets and spray, sugar or glucose solution, and syrup of ipecac. Stock some over-the-counter medicines including aspirin and acetaminophen (Tylenol). You will want about 1000 tablets of 500 mg. acetaminophen on hand. For children you'll want one bottle of acetaminophen liquid. You may also want to get 1000 tablets of diphenhydramine (Benadryl) as an antihistamine. Have on hand some Kaopectate or Pepto Bismol, 1000 milk of magnesia tablets, one pound of petrolatum, and one pound of zinc oxide. For fungal skin infections get some tolnaftate powder or about 45 grams of Tinactin. You may also want 1000 tablets of pseudoephedrine to battle allergies.

These are merely guidelines and suggestions, of course. We are not medical doctors, and we encourage you to talk with your family doctor and buy a good home health-care book so that you'll be fully prepared. You will no doubt want to add or delete items based on your family needs.

Treating Burns

Having these supplies, the next thing you'll want to consider is the actual treatments. We'll begin with burns, bites, infections, and frostbite, then we'll cover colds, coughs, allergies, constipation, diarrhea, fever, indigestion, and nausea.

As mentioned in earlier parts of this book, *fire is a major concern*. If at all possible, you want to avoid getting burned from fire and from touching hot things like pots and pans, or hot liquids, known as scalds. If you are with someone else who gets burned, remain calm. Determine the degree of burn—first-degree burns have no blisters, but they do have stinging pain and perhaps an inflamed area; second-degree burns produce a blister; and third-degree burns show charred skin and nasty-looking craters that can quickly get infected. The first treatment for all burns is to get the affected area submerged in clean, cold water for as long as it takes to decrease the pain. For a first-degree burn apply a dressing soaked in aloe vera—you might want to keep an aloe vera plant in the kitchen so you can simply break a leaf and smear the sap on the wound. As soon as possible expose the burn to the air. You'll want to keep the area moist, and a little salve will help achieve this.

For second-degree burns, break the blisters with a sterile needle and do not remove the deflated skin. A dressing soaked in aloe vera cream or honey is then applied. Keep the burn moist. Third-degree burns are life-threatening and really should get emergency medical attention, but that might not be a possibility. Get the burn into clean water—this takes out the sting, as long as the burn is underwater and out of the air. Do not cover the burn with butter or ointment. Moisture is needed for the first 24 hours. Understand that burned areas dry out very quickly and form painful dry scabs.

The primary problem with a third-degree burn is infection, so be very careful and keep the various implements you're using sterile. Boil the water before using it for cold soaks. Sterilize the container you are using for soaking the burns, and be sure you are wearing rubber gloves and applying sterile dressings. For the first few hours of treatment keep the burned area covered with a dressing moist with sterile cold water or aloe vera. Be careful the dressing does not stick to the wound.

You should see signs of healing in the first 48-hour period. Healing will take place at the bottom of a crater first. Once healing has begun, you may start a regular routine of applying a dressing soaked in aloe vera, honey, or tea tree oil. Change the dressings every two or three days. If the patient says the burn is not causing discomfort, leave well enough alone. In addition to dressing the wound, you'll want to give the patient plenty of fluids to drink, and you'll want to increase the amount of protein given to the patient. During the first 48 hours take the patient's temperature often—fever is a sign of infection. After the first two days, check the person's temperature daily. If infection occurs, seek professional help immediately.

Give the patient soothing tea. Do not sedate a burn victim with alcohol. Although you want to relieve pain and tension, you still need the person to be aware of sensation as much as possible. He or she needs to be able to feel what is happening and be able to tell you. Given time, care, and cleanliness, the wound will heal.

Winter Injuries

Y2K starts in the middle of winter. While the prospects of fires are high, especially in situations where open wood fires are being used to heat and cook and kerosene lamps are being used to light, we also need to consider what cold can do to the human body. Frostbite, which can set in either slowly or very quickly, will not concern people living in warmer climates, but it is a fact of outdoor life for people living in the northern United States and Canada. *Frostbite can be prevented by wearing layers of warm clothing, not smoking or drinking alcohol, and staying indoors as much as possible.*

Toes, fingers, ears, noses and chins are the areas most susceptible to frostbite. The danger signs to look for include initial pain, swelling, white skin, then numbness and eventually loss of function and absence of pain. It's possible that blisters might develop. The best advice is to heat the affected area by soaking in a tub consisting of an antiseptic solution such as hydrogen peroxide and warm water—no hotter than 104 degrees Fahrenheit. When the affected area becomes red, stop soaking. You do not want to rush the thawing process, for it should take about 45 minutes. After the soaking, keep the affected area elevated and do not massage it. Cover it from the cold.

You might think it's not possible to get insect bites in the winter, but it is. Bees are out in winter; they just aren't as visible as they are in the spring and summer. To fix bee stings, first remove the stinger, then cleanse the area with an antiseptic like hydrogen peroxide. If there is a lot of swelling, use cold salt-water soaks. Children will often suffer a minor shock from insect bites, especially bee bites, so give a child a cup of warm, soothing, sweet tea.

Insect and animal bites are fairly preventable. Avoiding dogs, cats, and other small animals will certainly reduce the chances of being bitten. For insects, keep foods and drinks tightly covered, avoid sweet-smelling colognes, wear an insect repellent, choose white or neutral colors to avoid bees, wear snug clothing, and don't go barefoot. You will also want to treat pets for fleas. Even with these precautions, you might still get bitten. If you are allergic to bees and other insect bites, make certain you pack medication in your emergency supplies.

In emergency situations, dogs are often hungry and frightened. Stay away from packs of roving dogs. Look for signs of rabies including frothing at the mouth and absence of fear in the dog. The treatment for animal bites begins with stopping the bleeding and assessing the degree of the bite. Keep your patient and yourself calm. Cleanse the wound by pouring clean, sterile water over the entire area. You want to remove dirt and debris prior to covering the wound, then soak the area in warm salt water for a few minutes to reduce the shock as well as to clean it. Now examine the wound: How deep is it? Is there torn muscle or is muscle fiber visible? Will the wound need suturing? Is any flesh missing? Did the dog tear the skin while shaking its head, or was it a bite-and-run situation?

If the bite is severe and it is possible to do so, get the victim to an emergency ward. Otherwise you can dress and cover the injury as you would any other. A large crater left by an animal tearing at the bite site is a serious problem—there is a good chance of infection, and healing is difficult. Do not pack the wound hole with dressing or pads, even if they are sterile. Packing it will cause the wound to dry out, and the dressings will stick inside. Close the wound carefully and dress it with a 4 x 4 pad. The next step is to apply zinc oxide under the dressing to hold the wound site together. Make sure it is not too tight. In the case of a large, gaping wound too big to close, you'll need to lay a dressing soaked in aloe vera across the whole wound and dress it so as to leave the injury site safe from invasion. During the treatment keep the patient calm. Over the next few days watch for signs of infection. As soon as possible, apply a covering of antiseptic ointment and expose the wound to the air when possible. A large bite wound heals slowly.

One concern of wounds and burns is the danger of infection. If you notice infection in a wound, you will want to soak it in a container of hot liquid. You want the liquid not uncomfortably hot, but still as hot as possible. Soak the infected area for 15 minutes, then transfer to cold liquid for 5 minutes. The point of this is to get the blood flowing and free up clogged areas around the wound. For most wounds use Epsom salts to aid in the drawing-out process (but do not use Epsom salts for infected burns). After soaking, redress the wound with a poultice—a soft mass of various ingredients with the consistency of a pudding. If there is pus, use a poultice made of grated soap and sugar. Later, when the dressing is removed, continue the soaks until the wound is cleaned out. Once the infection is gone, return to medications.

Coughs, Colds, and Allergies

There is no known cure for the common cold, but it's not life-threatening. *The accepted advice on colds and flu is to simply let them run their course and go away on their own.* Colds usually last about five or six days, and flu will last about three or four.

A solution of salt or borax water will cleanse the stopped nose and throat. Mix one teaspoon salt or borax in a pint of warm water and let stand for at least an hour. Shake well and use as a gargle. Also, placing a small amount in your palm and snorting the solution up your nose will help your passages clear. You might want to inhale eucalyptus for a stopped-up nose and bronchial tubes. Put ten drops of eucalyptus oil in a small saucer of hot water, place a towel over your head, and gently inhale.

There are three kinds of coughs. A productive cough brings up mucus or phlegm. A nonproductive cough is dry and doesn't bring up anything. A reflex cough comes from a problem somewhere else, like the ear or stomach. You'll want to treat the cause and soothe the irritation. Coughs are caused by allergy, infection, cigarette smoke, something stuck in your windpipe, or dry air. Inhale eucalyptus oil and camphor oil in steam over a bowl in order to get a soft coating into your throat. You can also smear the oil on your chest for constant inhaling. To keep your throat clear, gargle salt water.

Allergic reactions generally consist of watery eyes and sneezing. The first step in treating an allergy is to remove the cause of the irritation if you know what it is. If you have family members with allergies, make sure you store allergy medication for those emergencies. If you need to get a doctor's prescription, do so. Bathe swollen, irritated eyes in a solution of aloe vera juice and water.

Sore throats can manifest themselves in a number of ways, from mild, scratchy irritation to severe pain. The causes can be viral, fungal, or bacterial infection. Gargle salt water every few hours, drink plenty of warm tea and soup, and avoid spicy foods. For inflamed throats you'll want cold foods and liquids. Suck on a hard piece of candy, and take aspirin for pain.

Fevers usually indicate infection. Adults don't need to do anything if they feel OK, but if their temperature is above 104 degrees Fahrenheit, or if they don't feel good, they should drink plenty of liquids and avoid solid foods. Plenty of rest will help. If the fever continues, try sponge baths with warm water and take aspirin. Fever is more of a concern with children. Follow the same procedures, but begin if the child's temperature is 102 degrees or more.

Tummy Trouble

One of the most common problems during emergency situations is constipation, mainly due to tension and a change in diet. The causes for constipation are usually lack of fresh fruits and vegetables, lack of activity, and lack of fluids. The best remedy is to eat high-fiber foods such as bran, cereals, fresh fruits, and vegetables. Avoid sugar and dairy products. It's also a good idea to drink plenty of water and hot tea or coffee. You also want plenty of exercise.

The other common problem in emergency conditions is diarrhea. Preventive measures include washing your hands after you use the toilet, washing your hands before you cook, not sharing towels with others, and drying your hands with paper towels. One of the major causes of diarrhea is lack of clean water, though other causes include viral or bacterial infections, parasites, ingestion of bad food or water, emotional turmoil, and allergies. *Diarrhea can indicate infection in your intestines, so be sure of high hygiene standards.* Increase your fluid intake. For children, diarrhea can lead to dehydration. Use combinations of molasses and water to help restore nutrition. Also, barley water, brown rice water, and soybean water can be combined with molasses. These three liquids are created by boiling the substance—barley, brown rice, and soybeans—in water. Other liquids such as clear broth, weak tea with sugar, flat cola, 7-Up, or ginger ale are good and usually easy to digest. Reduce dairy products, fruits, and fruit juices. Increase salt intake and get rest.

Indigestion and nausea are normally caused by tainted food or drink. It will help to fast for several hours, drink some soothing mint tea, and take some garlic. Please note that all of the above information is meant as a guideline. There are obviously many things we did not cover, so we recommend you have two or three medical books on hand in addition to a first-aid book.

The Two- to Three-Day Plan

Hopefully, in a two- or three-day crisis you and your family won't need any medical attention, but we still recommend you have a first-aid kit and medical books handy just in case. *The major strategy should be prevention.* Be careful when cooking and preparing a meal. Practice basic hygiene. Be cautious with fires and fuels. Use common sense, and you should be OK.

Be sure you provide for any special needs and medications you or your family have, and realize it's very possible you will not be able to get immediate medical attention. There is also a good chance the pharmacy will be closed.

Unlike other disasters, Y2K shouldn't cause much physical destruction. The very fact that there is less material destruction indicates there should be fewer medical emergencies.

The One-Month Plan

Medical supplies will become far more important if the Y2K emergency lasts for 30 days. This is especially true if you or anyone in your family requires prescription medications or specialized medical attention. Talk with your family members about what to do if they face a medical emergency. How will they get to a hospital? Whom will they tell? What steps should they take? If your family has discussed the situation, you will all be better prepared to deal with the confusion of doctors, nurses, and hospitals.

Because more time is involved, there is also the greater probability of accidents and other emergencies. The probability also increases with the number of persons and the age of the people. As noted earlier, children and the elderly are more prone to health problems than others. *Prevention is still a key, but supplies are important.* If you believe the emergency will last a month, be sure to have a well-stocked medicine cabinet.

The One-Year Plan

If you believe the Y2K crisis will last a year or longer, you need to take much more serious precautions. It's imperative you know your family's situation and needs. You will also require the cooperation and support of your doctor for getting drugs. You'll want extra prescriptions for regular medications, so you'll need to consider your budget. Provide for the basics first, then get additional drugs. Make sure the drugs you get have at least a year's shelf life—there's no sense wasting money on medications which are bad when you need them.

If you or anyone in your family has any of the following conditions, you need to be especially concerned: acute or chronic respiratory illnesses, heart ailments, epilepsy, unstable or juvenile diabetes, dependenced, upon tube feeding, urinary catheters, colostomies, dialysis dependence, and tracheotomies. Talk with your doctor about creating a medical plan. You may need to provide special procedures for the frail, the elderly, and the handicapped. Get medical advice about the best way to handle these conditions if no medical or pharmaceutical attention is available.

Additionally, you will need more than just drugs and supplies—*you'll need knowledge.* You might want to enroll in a first-aid session or basic life-support class, or even audit some college courses in medicine. The more you know about medical procedures, the better off you and your family will be in the event of an emergency.

Finally, realize the human race survived for many centuries without modern medicine. Practice daily healthy habits and common-sense prevention, and you should be able to survive, too.

YOUR Y2K PLANNING GUIDE

Ten Steps to Prepare for a Medical Emergency

1. Realize that emergency health care may be difficult, if not impossible, to get.
2. Know your own and your family's present health conditions.
3. Make a list of medical supplies you might need.
4. Practice wellness and prevention.
5. Have a good first-aid book.
6. Stockpile medical supplies.
7. Know treatments for most common medical emergencies.
8. Practice medical treatment with your kids.
9. Know what you need to do and have for people with special medical needs.
10. Take classes in first aid.

TEN

Safety Solutions

According to the police, the 911 emergency system is often abused. As much as ten percent of all calls to your local 911 center are either prank calls, hang-ups, or nonemergency calls. The following words were recorded by a 911 operator in Marathon County, Wisconsin: "Yeah. I just locked my keys and I ran in the store real quick, and I accidentally left my keys in the car." Obviously, misplaced keys do not warrant an emergency call. Yet in a Y2K crisis, you can expect a definite increase in such calls (assuming, of course, the telephone system still works). In stressful situations, people often do not think clearly nor act appropriately. An overwhelmed 911 system will have a major impact on the efficiency and speed of our emergency services.

Add to this the fact that 911 is heavily dependent upon computers. If there is massive computer failure, it could well affect the service we've come to expect. Embedded chips are a real concern, since police and fire departments rely on all sorts of equipment with embedded chips, including radios, radio substations, electronic locks, elevators, conventional phones,

What's Ahead

- **Safe at Home**

- **Neighbors, Locks, and Defense**

- **Martial Law**

- **The Two- to Three-Day Plan**

- **The One-Month Plan**

- **The One-Year Plan**

- **The Y2K Planning Guide**

cell phones, CCTV cameras, radar speed detectors, photo surveillance equipment, traffic-light controllers, sprinkler systems,
and nearly all fire alarms. The pervasive nature of Y2K suggests
so many different areas will be disrupted that all safety and
emergency services—including fire, police, and medical units—
will be rendered impotent. You will need to have planned solutions for a wide range of difficult conditions.

Safe at Home

Prevention and planning are key factors in protecting
your family from a variety of potential life-threatening circumstances. What will you do if there is a fire? If there is looting in
your neighborhood? If a gang of thugs wants your food supplies
or firewood? It's very difficult to imagine some of these potential
problems, but to some degree we consider possible threats to our
safety regularly in everyday life. Even now city dwellers realize
there are some risks in daily life. Crimes happen all the time.
The crime rate in America is astonishing: 13,992,000 violent
crimes were committed in 1994 (the most recent data available).

People have burglar alarms because of the potential threat
of crime, we have smoke detectors and fire alarms to protect us
from fire disasters, and the 911 service was established in 1968
because we knew our lives were filled with crisis situations.
Although we might not like to admit it, we know safety is an
important element in our lives.

Therefore the first step in preparing for your safety is to *take
stock of your current situation.* Do you use smoke detectors or fire
alarms? Do they work? How recently were the batteries
inspected? Even though there may be an electrical blackout,
long-lasting batteries were designed for such appliances as
smoke detectors, so they should still work. You cannot rely on
the fire alarm to contact your fire department in a Y2K emergency, but you can still expect it to warn you of a fire hazard.
Have you and your family ever done a fire drill? Do you know
where the exits are, and is there a safe way out of most rooms in

your dwelling? Do you have fire extinguishers? If you do, when was the last time they were charged? Does everyone in your family know how to use them?

Do you have a security system? Does it rely on electricity and telephone communication systems? If it works on batteries, have they been checked recently? Again, don't expect the burglar alarm to bring the police in a Y2K disaster, though it might be enough to ward off criminals. The purpose of burglar alarms in general is to act as a deterrent.

Do you keep many valuables in your home? If so, do you have a fireproof safe? In the year 2000, what's valuable might change in its meaning. Currently it means cash and jewelry, but it might mean firewood and pure water. How secure are your windows and doors? Do you have limited access from the outside? Do you have bars over your windows? Does your home have dead bolts? Do you have a guard dog? Have you ever considered owning a gun? What do you currently have or do that protects you from crime? In the last chapter we discussed the importance of first aid and medical preparedness. In this chapter we want to ask you to assess your safety preparedness.

Neighbors, Locks, and Defense

There are three things which you can do to your present home to make it safer and more secure in a crisis, whether you live in the country, suburbia, or the inner city. First, *get to know your neighbors*—not just the civil nod, but a real relationship. Have them over for dinner. In an apartment building with lots of transient tenants, it is difficult to establish relationships. In such a case, at least establish a working relationship with the apartment manager. People who know each other can unite together for the common defense and help one another in providing for basic needs. You will be safer and stronger in a group than by yourself.

Second, *install dead bolts on all your exterior doors and make sure all your windows have working locks.* You might even consider establishing a "safe room" in your home—one room which is the most secure with heavy locking doors, including a lock on the inside, good ventilation, and protective supplies.

Third, *learn to defend yourself in a way which is congruent with your personal philosophy*. This does not mean you have to buy a gun, though we believe this is exactly the reason our founding fathers assured us of the constitutional right to bear arms. However, we understand many people are not comfortable owning a gun. Realize there are other self-defense alternatives, including martial arts, mace, and baseball bats. It's important that you and your family take stock of the potential dangers and make plans to find solutions. You need to think about your philosophy regarding self-protection. If you or your family are threatened by criminals, what will you do? How far are you willing to go? Would you rather run than fight, or hide and hope the danger goes away? It's possible there may be heavy disagreement in your family about what's appropriate and ethical to do in protecting yourself and your children. Whatever your feelings on the subject, it's imperative you all agree on what you will do. Talk about it—propose several different scenarios and ask for thoughts on each one. Some scenarios might be repulsive and scary, but it's better to know how to react in case they do happen, than to not be prepared and hesitate in your reaction.

Martial Law

There are those people who believe in the possibility of extreme Y2K computer failures causing the collapse of urban society. Their argument sounds like this: Without banking, utilities, communication systems, and transportation, most cities and even small towns will become hellish nightmares. *They contend such conditions will require the federal government to declare martial law, and there are some indications the U.S. government is preparing to do exactly that.* Under the cover of the phrases "critical infrastructure protection" and "cyberterrorism," the government is setting up rapid deployment forces designed to provide order in American cities. In July 1996, President Clinton signed an order to create the Presidential Commission on Critical

Infrastructure Protection (PCCIP). Since late 1997, plans to establish martial law have been in effect. The Army has created special emergency-response divisions made up of National Guard units and reserve units.

Testimony was presented by Major General Edward Philbin, executive director of the National Guard Association of the United States, to the Senate Special Committee on the Year 2000 Technology Problem on October 2, 1998. He offered the opinions of the association and its members, who are the commissioned and warrant officers of the Army and Air National Guard. His words:

> Considering the possibilities of a large scale disruption of governmental, commercial and other routine daily activities, it is certain that the National Guard will be among the first organizations activated to assist in the revitalization of the nation's computer-dependent infrastructure. As with hurricanes, floods, and other incidents requiring a quick reaction by a well-trained and equipped on-site team, no other organization will be able to respond in support of police, fire fighting and other civilian emergency responders, to major crisis situations that may be caused by Y2K disruptions as well as the National Guard. The National Guard's practiced interaction with state and local organizations and its connections to the National Command Authority provide a unique emergency response capability not found in any other federal or state organization.

To many people, the possibility of martial law is reassuring. It means we will still be protected from outlaw crime and have emergency services assured. A series of executive orders which go back over 30 years are in reserve, ready to be announced and enforced by the president. In a Y2K crisis, the public will demand emergency actions. But can the armed services carry out such assignments? It too relies on computers, and it too is not yet Y2K compliant. Major General Edward Philbin, went on to state:

> We must be certain that the National Guard will not itself be a victim of any Y2K disruption. All National Guard units in 3,200 locations throughout the nation, must possess computer dependent equipment that is Y2K compliant. Responding to the consequences of a Y2K disruption will be futile if the National Guard's operations are plagued by the very consequences the Guard is attempting to manage. It is critical that the Y2K response requirements of the National Guard be fully funded to ensure that it is able to respond quickly and effectively to the needs of the community.

Some individuals regard the idea of martial law as a threat to the Constitution, and worry we will lose our rights to an intrusive federal government. The idea of armed National Guardsmen patrolling neighborhoods is disturbing in America, and we do not know what would happen to our civil rights if such a condition existed. In all emergency situations prior to Y2K, once order was restored the National Guard left . . . but this is an entirely different situation, since there is the possibility it might be a long lasting national crisis.

The Two- to Three-Day Plan

As noted elsewhere, a two- or three-day crisis is more of a nuisance than anything else. If you have prepared for a short-term emergency, you will be more concerned about survival basics such as food and water supplies and keeping warm than security and safety issues. But to some degree this depends upon where you are located. In the inner city especially, it might be wise to *secure your dwelling and your property so it cannot be easily invaded or robbed.* Single women in particular need to consider taking their safety precautions seriously.

You need to inspect your doors and windows. Make sure you have a dead bolt and other locking mechanisms that will keep you safe. If you don't have a dead bolt, consider having one installed. You can hire a locksmith to do this for you, or you can do this yourself. In some areas, organizations like Neighborhood Watch will inspect your home to see how secure it is and make safety recommendations. If this kind of program is available to you and you currently don't know how secure your home is, take advantage of the opportunity to learn.

If you do have emergency supplies, consider hiding them or keeping them in a separate locked area. You do not want your supplies left unprotected and accessible to strangers. If you decide to store anything outside, we recommend you keep it locked and hidden. If you are heating and/or cooking with firewood, you will want to consider keeping your fuel secure as well. Hiding a cord of wood might be difficult, so try keeping it in a locked shed. Use heavy-duty locks with keys (combination locks are difficult when being used by several family members) and check to make sure the hasps on the door are tamperproof. The lock will be of little use if the hasp can be unscrewed or cut open easily. In a short-term emergency the problem of theft is minimal, but keeping firewood secure is still a reasonable idea.

During the actual emergency, try to be inconspicuous when getting your outdoor stores. It's preferable if people do not know what you have stored or where you are hiding it. If you must travel in an urban area, remain as inconspicuous as possible. Dress warmly but simply, since you do not want to attract attention. Remove any jewelry before beginning your trip, and by all means avoid areas were there is looting. Move slowly and make no suspicious moves— you don't want to be shot at by either looters, the National Guard, or police. Appreciate the level of tension where you are traveling. In a small town there probably won't be much stress or many problems, but in large cities, there most certainly will be.

The One-Month Plan

The longer the duration of the crisis, the more panic-stricken and desperate people will become. If you have warmth, water, food, and are reasonably comfortable, *how will you deal with people who want you to share your goods with them?* Can you say no? Do you have enough extra to give to other people?

This may sound cold and calculating, but you need to think about these issues now. How much are you going to store, and who is it intended for? Make a list of those people you will help, and be sure you have enough to share with them. Unless you have a tremendous amount of space and a big budget, you will need to keep this list fairly small. What will you do when you are approached by a friend or a relative not on your list? Will you make exceptions? Can you deny them? If you don't help a friend, are you willing to deal with the repercussions? How much responsibility are you willing to take?

Finding answers for questions like these is difficult, so discuss them as a family. Besides yourself, whom do you need to be responsible for? Is it wrong for you to have more supplies than others? (If you are prepared and others aren't, this will certainly become an important issue, and you can expect many unprepared people.) What will you do if outside forces, either good or bad, compel you to share your goods? It is one thing to be charitable, and an entirely different thing to be forced to be charitable. A martial-law situation might create just such possibilities. Is it wrong to sell food to the starving? If you have plenty of extra food stores, should you be allowed to make a profit off the misfortunes of others? Is it right to protect yourself and your family from harm? Is it wrong to let strangers suffer and possibly die of starvation so you and your family might survive? Is it right to kill attackers if they threaten you with harm? When does a threat become life-threatening? If you encounter intruders, how will you interpret their actions? Will you assume their intent is to do you harm?

Are you willing to buy a gun? Guns are a very controversial issue. Do we want our survival to rely on guns and brute force? Guns are also dangerous, since their only purpose is to kill. In a wilderness situation the target might be game and the purpose of the kill to help procure food for survival, but in an urban situation the only purpose is to kill attackers, whether they be wild dogs or outlaw thugs. And who exactly is a thug? Is it someone who wants what you have? How do you determine bad guys from good guys? As a Christian, think carefully through these issues before investing in a gun.

Unfortunately, guns sometimes kill the innocent. Most of the time the killing is caused by an accidental firing and the victim is a child, so if you decide you must keep a gun, make sure gun safety is practiced. Have all the adults in your family take a class in gun use, so if something happens to the gun owner, others can still use it. Many state and local governments provide these classes for a minimal fee, sometimes even free of charge as part of a gun-registration procedure. An untrained and scared individual with a loaded gun is dangerous to everyone. Training gives the individual confidence and reduces his chance of hurting himself or an innocent party. A good class will cover all the basics including safety procedures, cleaning, loading, and firing. Above all, make sure the keys to the lock are only given to responsible adults.

The One-Year Plan

The one-year scenario assumes the collapse of civilization as we know it and a return to the Old West. If Y2K continues for a full year or longer, the last place you want to be is in a city, simply because of the sheer number of people involved and the degree of desperation which will ensue. There will be gangs and individual marauders. Of course, they already exist in every city today. Police in New York City believe gangs and career criminals make up about eight percent of the population—roughly 640,000 people. Many of these people are in and out of jail so frequently it seems the criminal population is actually larger than it really is. A severe Y2K emergency could cause the number of gangs to increase, and a city without a working police force, a city in which night is truly dark, and a city in which no alarms work will attract criminal activity. We already know to expect looting in a "normal" emergency situation, so think of the opportunities for the immoral in a more intense crisis.

This does not mean the country life is without its problems. One obvious danger is the threat of intruders from outside the community. If most of the city dwellers leave the city, where will they go? They will target small towns. The population of a normally small town might explode over the period of a year just from immigration. Another problem is a community's acceptance of you. If you have just recently moved to the town within the past year or so, how is your status that much different from those who try to move into the community after January 1, 2000? Are you a newcomer and the others intruders?

In many small communities there is a reliance on one or two industries. If those fail because of Y2K, what will happen to the townspeople? How will that affect the lifestyle of the community? Moving out of the city might solve one set of problems, but it might introduce another set. If you consider leaving urban life behind, we suggest you move to a place in which you already have connections. At least this will lessen the perception of you as unwelcome.

In a small town you might want to consider helping to establish a patrol program to assist and support the local police. Enlist people who are community-minded. Do not arm the patrol, but use two-way radios to communicate and call for needed help. Provide training for all members of the patrol program. Create some kind of uniform, even just a silk-screened T-shirt with the word *Patrol* printed on it. The uniform will help to identify the members and create team spirit. You might involve teenagers in the patrol, since it's a good activity and keeps the teenagers from becoming bored. At least provide other structured activities for teens—boredom often seduces them into joining gangs and committing crimes.

We have tried to avoid an alarmist tone in this chapter, and hopefully in the entire book. However, contemplating unpleasant and even life-threatening possibilities is unfortunately a part of being prepared for such an emergency. As we've said elsewhere, it's far better to imagine negative conditions and have solutions for them than to avoid the subject entirely and not be ready.

YOUR Y2K PLANNING GUIDE

20 Questions for Creating Safety During Y2K

1. You might not be able to depend on emergency services like the fire department, the police department, or medical emergency wards. *Whom will you turn to?*
2. Prevention and planning are key factors in protecting your family from a variety of potential life-threatening circumstances. *Has your family discussed safety?*
3. The first step in preparing for your safety is to take stock of your current situation. *How safe are you now?*
4. Know about fire safety and prevention. *What will you do in case of fire?*
5. Know about home and personal security. *What will you do in case of home invasion?*
6. Know about first aid and emergency medical treatments. *What will you do in case of injury?*
7. Get to know your neighbors. *How can you make friends?*
8. Install dead bolts and check to make sure all windows lock. *Do you have dead bolts and window locks?*
9. Learn to defend yourself in a way that is congruent with your personal philosophy. *Could you use deadly force to defend yourself or your family?*
10. Consider the possibility and impact of martial law. *What would happen if the National Guard is keeping the peace in your town?*
11. Lock and possibly hide your emergency supplies, especially your firewood, food, and water. *How do you plan to secure your supplies?*
12. Practice common sense if you need to travel—keep a low profile. *If we had to travel, what precautions would we take?*
13. Make a list of people you will help and then make sure you have enough to share with those people. *Whom will you help, and what will you say to those you choose not to help?*
14. Consider getting a gun and taking a gun class. *Do you want a gun in your house?*
15. Learn how to shoot your gun. *Do you feel confident using your gun?*
16. Learn how to clean it and take care of it. *Are you taking good care of your weapons?*
17. Make sure guns are kept in a locked, dry, cool area. Store replacement parts, ammunition, and cleaning supplies for the gun. *Is your gun safe right now?*
18. Train others in the use of the gun. *If not you, who could use it?*
19. Consider leaving the city and moving to a small town. *Where would you go?*
20. Realize the possible difficulties of adjustment to a small town. *Would moving to a small town be right for your family?*

ELEVEN

Communication Concerns

I n both *Spontaneous Healing* and *Eight Weeks to Optimal Healing*, Dr. Andrew Weil recommends taking a "news fast"—a day without broadcast news. In his opinion, the constant exposure to negative, depressing news is unhealthy. The Y2K situation may not allow us the freedom of such a choice, but rather may force us to be without news for a weekend . . . or perhaps much longer.

While we may not like broadcast news, we rely on it. Millions of commuters depend on traffic and weather reports just to get to and from work. Other people rely on updated news reports to make business decisions. The stock market bases its success or failure on its response to national and global news. While not as immediate as the electronic media, print is a vital element in supplying us with a more detailed source of facts and opinions. For many of us a balance of radio, television, and newspaper information is a major aspect of how we

---

What's Ahead

- **Y2K and the Media**

- **Personal Communicaiton**

- **Your Reliance on Communication**

- **Anticipating Problems**

- **The Two- to Three-Day Plan**

- **The One-Month Plan**

- **The One-Year Plan**

- **Your Y2K Planning Guide**

form our worldview. Without these various media we would only have personal gossip and thirdhand knowledge.

Even gossip requires a conduit, and for most of us that means the telephone and, to a lesser degree, the United States mail. Many of us are beginning to find we depend upon secondary aspects of telecommunications like e-mail and faxes. Remove the telephone, and we would suffer a tremendous sense of alienation and isolation.

How could Y2K cripple our communication systems? Apart from the reliance on electricity, there are many ways.

Y2K and the Media

Radio and television news is normally recorded by microphone or TV camera, then mixed and edited in a control room. Next it is transmitted via satellite or telephone line to local stations, and finally broadcast over a transmitter. *Much of this equipment contains embedded computers, which are vulnerable to Y2K.* Dating of material for archival and retrieval purposes is a common practice, but whenever computers and dates are involved, the possibility of Y2K bugs undoubtedly exists.

Oddly, the reliance on in-studio performers (announcers) is more strongly felt in the news programs of radio and TV than in the entertainment portion. Entertainment programs are usually recorded long before they are broadcast, but news programs create a sense of immediacy by being given by a live human. If transportation is impeded by Y2K keeping the announcer from reaching the studio, or if business management has problems getting paychecks to the employees, the result is greatly delayed news or even no news at all.

Transmission of news from the field—wherever it's taking place—to the studio is also susceptible to Y2K problems. Usually field correspondents transmit the appropriate information by telephone, satellite, or some other medium to the studio. Broadcast news has come to depend upon sophisticated satellite-supported transmission systems. With no telephone or satellite connections, "live" news is dead.

We recognize that most TV and radio broadcasting is sponsored by commercial messages, and these advertisements are carefully scheduled and synchronized to fit correctly into the rest of the broadcasting schedule. This entire process is heavily computerized, and the software which manages it relies on date calculations. The immediate result of Y2K failure on this procedure might be commercial-free broadcasting. That might be all right for a few days, but after longer periods of time the advertisers will stop paying for unaired commercials. This means no income, and that means the stations will not be able to afford to operate. The impact of this will probably be felt on smaller companies rather than on larger ones.

The print media consisting of newspapers and magazines will also feel the effect of Y2K. Like all other businesses that rely on computers for invoicing and billing, there will be some negative repercussions from programs which are not compliant. The impact on billing would be seen especially in the area of subscriptions—newspaper and magazines subscriptions may appear to have never been paid or are years overdue, thus causing the automated system to terminate the subscription.

Like with other products, distribution of the periodicals may be affected by Y2K. Magazines and newspapers rely on a convoluted network of planes, trains, and trucks to get their product out. If something goes wrong with this system, the publication won't arrive. Paper, ink, and other supplies involve distribution problems from the receiving side. Without these materials the publications have nothing to print on or with. Yes, stockpiling is a possibility, but the supplies are so bulky and costly that most publishers rely on a just-in-time operating procedure. Additionally, the situation is complicated by the fact that many publications are created in one location and then broadcast electronically to various other locations around the nation and the world for regional distribution and printing. So newspapers and magazines are reliant upon the satellite and telecommunications network for distributing their merchandise.

Publications also depend upon the telecommunications network for getting news reports from the field. Real time immediacy is not as pressing with print media as it is with electronic media, but if the information is delayed more than a day, the result is not deemed newsworthy.

Advertising also supports print news just as it does broadcast news. The advertising material comes in a variety of forms, and much of it is computer-dependent. The issue of immediacy is a little different than it is for radio and TV commercials, in that a newspaper might be able to suspend its printing for a little while until its major advertiser manages to deliver the copy and graphics. The more reliant the publication's advertising department is on computers, the more likely it is to be tainted by Y2K problems.

Then there's the issue of printing. Modern periodicals are partially if not completely dependent upon computers for phototypesetting, page composition, graphic design, and other production details. For bigger publishers this often involves very costly specialized computers. Determining Y2K compliance would call for a case-by-case analysis. Smaller companies might easily use the more standard desktop software and operating systems. If they do, they are not immune to Y2K infection.

Personal Communication

As individuals we rely on two important systems for our personal communications: telephones and mail. Of course, you could probably survive without phones for individual communication, but most businesses could not. Speaking before the U.S. Senate Committee on Commerce, Science, and Transportation, Federal Communications Commission Chairman William E. Kennard said,

> If we have major network outages due to Year 2000, many small- and medium-sized businesses could find themselves in dire economic straits. Many must rely on only one telecommunications carrier. So if their phone network or their data network goes out, they have to

close down. And many small businesses don't have large reserves, so if the problem persists for a few days, they could be out of business.

It's very possible that some phone companies, especially the smaller ones—about 1400 of which serve many rural and insular areas of the United States—will have severe problems and could be inoperable for a long period of time. Most phone companies are currently working hard to become Y2K compliant, but that doesn't mean they will be.

The FCC thinks foreign telecommunications companies, particularly those in developing countries in Africa and Asia, will have difficulty providing service after December 31, 1999. According to Kennard, "This could have a huge impact on international trade, foreign investment, the global economy and even national security . . . These countries are only now becoming aware of the Year 2000 problem and they lack the resources to fully address it." It seems unlikely that all phone service will stop, but it is very possible some will. What is the status of your supplier? Is it Y2K compliant? How many phone companies are involved in your service? Is your long-distance service different from your cellular service? Is your cellular service different from your local service? The advantage of many competitive phone companies means you can have different suppliers for different services, and in a Y2K meltdown this is desirable. It means you have a better chance of getting some service.

There are three elements of telephone service that are exposed to Y2K contamination: the network switches, PBX (the private branch exchange systems which control the inside telecommunications in most big businesses), and the financial/administrative network within the "carrier" companies. Switches are susceptible to Y2K because dating is part of their recording procedure. Network switches are the devices which establish the connection between your phone and another phone whenever you make or take a call. In fact, usually several switches are employed in a dialogue unless both speakers live in the same local area. The greater the distance between the two parties, the more switches there are involved. International calls will easily involve several switches, and these switches may be made by different companies, some compliant and some not.

Many businesses and government offices rely on the PBX, a kind of elaborate switch which relays numerous calls within one center. A single PBX is likely to handle thousands of calls daily for one organization. Many of the companies which employ a PBX don't upgrade it often, and the result is a workable system until January 1, 2000. In addition, almost all phone companies have computer systems which handle internal marketing, administrative matters, financial operations, billing, record-keeping, and scheduling of phone installations and repairs. All of these functions are date-sensitive information and therefore exposed to the Y2K problem.

Your Reliance on Communication

Like the telecommunications industry and most other businesses, shipping and postal carriers have elaborate billing, marketing, and other business applications in their computer programs. A Y2K problem in these systems probably wouldn't cause the carrier to shut down immediately, but it could cause billing problems and other administrative troubles. Another aspect of the shipping industry is the issue of transportation. All of the major shipping and postal carriers have their own air fleet. Y2K could ground air traffic, including cargo and package transport.

All of the major shippers, including the United States Postal System (USPS), have sophisticated computer systems to schedule, route, and control the movement of packages from pickup to delivery. From its origin to its final destination, a parcel will usually spend part of its time in a pick-up truck, a delivery truck, local offices in the city of origin and the city of destination, one or more airplanes, and one or more dispatching centers. The computer and tracking systems that schedule and coordinate all of this information are extremely complex and vulnerable to Y2K disruptions.

You need to assess your reliance on communication. *Begin by asking yourself and your family what your specific needs are.* How important is broadcast news to you? Do you rely on the electronic media to run your business? Do you rely on the radio for commuting? Many of us do, but in an emergency situation we may not be going to work as often as usual. Do you need both the radio and the TV? For most of us, one source is enough. If television is unavailable for any reason, including the likelihood of a power outage, you have the alternative of getting news broadcasts on your battery-operated radio.

In all probability, not all sources of news will be knocked out for the same time. If TV doesn't work, radio might. News is often the same no matter what station you turn to, so if your favorite station isn't broadcasting you will want to find another station. Even in the extremely unlikely circumstances that all American broadcasts are down, there are other broadcasts from other parts of the world. In the Y2K emergency, immediate news broadcasts might become very important for the latest information about disruptions to transportation, banking, and government services. We suggest you get a battery-operated radio and extra long-lasting batteries. Make sure the batteries are fully charged. You may want to consider getting a shortwave radio or a radio which is solar-powered or even hand-powered. Use the radio sparingly to extend its life.

Could you live without newspapers and magazines for a weekend? Could you survive without them for a month or a year? Your answers to these questions will depend upon your need for current, detailed information. For most of us, magazines are more for entertainment than for facts. Newspapers offer more details than the electronic media, but in an emergency, less-detailed information might be enough.

What will you and your family do if the telephone doesn't work? How will that affect your life? You might want to analyze your phone time. In a normal day how much of your time is spent on the phone for business reasons? How much for social reasons? If the phone was off for several days, could you survive? How many long-distance calls do you make? Of those long-distance calls, what proportion is for personal use and what proportion is for business? The most important use of a telephone is for life-threatening emergency situations, so you might consider getting a CB radio in case the phone isn't available.

When was the last time you wrote a letter to someone? How much do you mail? For conventional mail we send letters and bills, and receive subscriptions, and most of us depend upon the USPS. If we are shipping freight, we might turn to other carriers like UPS or FedEx. Do you use private carriers like FedEx and UPS at work, or do you rely more on the United States Postal System? Is your use of carriers for personal reasons or business reasons? Is immediate overnight service a crucial part of your business? Do you currently use e-mail more than standard mail? If you do, understand that e-mail is vulnerable because of its reliance on computers, telephone service, and electricity. The same thing can be said of faxes. So take a careful look at your life. Our guess is you rely heavily on communication.

Anticipating Problems

Once you and your family have established your reliance on different forms of communication, the next step is to *consider your communication options.* One possibility is to reduce your need for external communication. Another is to consider the importance of redundant sources, keeping access to as many different information services as possible. TV and radio provide many different stations, so you should have several sources for news. If all electronic media is down, turn to print news. You might want to anticipate problems by getting several subscriptions to different newspapers, then be sure your subscriptions are paid in advance.

You should be able to find news somewhere. The possibility of every news source going out at the same time is slim, but if your career and lifestyle depend upon timely, uninterrupted delivery of news, the more redundancy you have the better prepared you are. Better head to the outdoor store to pick up that battery-operated or solar-powered radio.

By all means, anticipate telephone problems. Consider getting a cellular phone, if you don't already have one. Also make sure the cell phone battery is fully charged, and that it is served by a different company than your regular phone. You are trying to create a backup system for communicating, so redundancy is crucial. If you have several cell phones, and large families often do, have each one served by a different company. If possible make sure all your phone services are from larger companies. Big corporations are more likely to have their systems Y2K compliant than smaller companies, and they are likely to get back on-line more quickly if they do go down. If your phone is crucial to your business, have multiple lines operated by several companies. Express your concerns about phone communications in 2000 with your most frequently called people, so that your clients and customers are aware of the potential for problems. If they are willing, establish alternative communication systems like walkie-talkies or CB radios.

You should also anticipate mail-carrier problems. Ship the really important business packages long before January 1, 2000. Let your business associates know the possibility of problems after that date, and your intention to get things to them however you need to do so. Realize the Christmas season is busy even under normal circumstances, and perhaps many cautious people may attempt to avoid potential problems in 2000 by mailing early. This means you should mail even earlier this fall. Of course, this strategy also applies to your personal mailing.

Another way to anticipate problems is to contact the various carriers and ask if they are Y2K compliant. Remember though, even if their systems are compliant, the dependency upon so many different factors does not mean they aren't susceptible to Y2K disruptions. If transportation is severely affected, mail distribution will be also. If blackouts occur, they will impact all businesses.

The Two- to Three-Day Plan

A short-lived emergency of three days will probably not change your normal communication practices significantly.

Services might be slower and some will not work, but you will be able to survive the crisis.

Having backup services established—multiple phones, multiple news services, and multiple carriers—and anticipating problems will make things a little easier. If you have friends or relatives you would expect to call to wish a "Happy New Year," know that either your phone or their phone might not be functioning. If your business office hasn't bothered to upgrade its PBX system, be aware you may be without telephone service the next workday. If you have friends and family scattered about the nation or the world, express your concerns about contacting them after January 1. Brainstorm ways of getting in touch with them, or contemplate less contact until the crisis is finished.

The One-Month Plan

A month without telephone and mail service is very serious. Most business operations will shut down if they can't communicate with their customers, vendors, and employees. Small- and medium-sized companies with minimal cash reserves could find themselves in real trouble because they can't get payments by mail. Larger organizations might be able to survive a bit better, but expect layoffs until problems are solved. Imagine the disaster a month-long telephone outage would cause on Wall Street!

In this scenario, the importance of backups increases considerably. If possible have additional cell phones with different services to back up other cell phones and conventional phone lines. Make sure you have well-charged batteries for all your phones, and plan to use them only for truly important calls.

Have access to as many different mail carriers as possible, which is much easier in a large city than in a small town. If the United States Postal System isn't working, maybe UPS or FedEx or yet another carrier will be. Although most of these carriers ship freight primarily, they will also carry correspondence.

For external news you will probably depend most upon a battery-powered radio. Use the radio sparingly. Additional radios are a good idea, but make sure you have well-charged batteries for them. Understand the strategy of redundant news services and provide for this tactic the best way you can, determined in part by your budget and location.

The One-Year Plan

A year-long crisis will mean a significant change in the way we live and in the way we communicate. It is unlikely all news sources will be down for a full year, but you may not be able to receive them if you live in an isolated area, if you've run out of batteries, or if you have had billing and distribution troubles. Look for other suppliers of phone and mail services if the ones you rely on are no longer operating. The good thing about deregulation in the telecommunications industry is the increased number of carriers available. There are several options from which to receive service, and we doubt that all phone companies and mail carriers will be inoperative.

As suggested many times, the more you can anticipate problems, the better prepared you will be. The more you communicate your worries to your family, friends, and business associates about communication and other areas of concern, the better you all will be.

YOUR Y2K PLANNING GUIDE

15 Communication Considerations

1. Realize the likelihood that broadcast news will be affected by Y2K.
2. Realize the likelihood that print news will be affected by Y2K.
3. Realize the likelihood that phone service will be affected by Y2K.
4. Realize the likelihood that mail carriers will be affected by Y2K.
5. Assess your reliance on communication.
6. Ask yourself and your family what your specific needs are.
7. What will you and your family do if the telephone doesn't work?
8. Consider getting additional cell phones and a variety of servers.
9. Consider getting a CB radio.
10. Limit the use of battery-operated radios and phones.
11. Consider a variety of mail carriers.
12. Consider limiting your communication needs.
13. Let friends, family, and business associates know about your concerns.
14. Ask your present communication providers if they are Y2K compliant.
15. If necessary, switch to companies which are Y2K compliant.

TWELVE

Transportation Troubles

Don't go home for the holidays at the end of 1999 unless you're planning to stay at least a month. No, we don't believe airplanes will fall from the skies, but we do believe there could be quite a bit of adversity affecting traveling in every form—from ships to buses to trains to planes to automobiles. How will you get from here to there after January 1, 2000?

Depending upon the size of your family and where you live, you might have several cars. Take stock of what you have and what you need to do for transportation before making the decision to travel. You need to consider how vulnerable your vehicles are, how safe your family feels, and how important it is that you take a trip during a potentially dangerous time.

Y2K and Your Automobile

The most common mode of transportation in the United States is the car. There are currently 100

What's Ahead

- **Y2K and Your Automobile**

- **Public Transportation**

- **Air Travel During Y2K**

- **Shipping and Handling**

- **Making Wise Travel Choices**

- **The Two- to Three-Day Plan**

- **The One-Month Plan**

- **The One-Year Plan**

- **Your Y2K Planning Guide**

million on the roads. The average American drives about 1000 miles a month or 12,000 miles yearly. We drive to work, to shop, and to play. How could Y2K impede you? If you're driving a 1968 Volkswagen Beetle you probably won't have any problems with your car, but as we stated earlier, there is genuine concern about newer vehicles. Embedded chips might cause problems after January 1, and *the standard newer car has about 50 microprocessors*. Some of these are basically inactive, but others provide control over such things as regulating the mixture of air and fuel in the carburetor, inflating air bags, and turning on alarms and lights. If any of these computer systems fail, the troubles could be either harmless or hazardous. A series of alarms going off would be more aggravating than dangerous, but an air bag that fails to inflate could mean the difference between life and death.

Ask your mechanic or dealer about the Y2K compliance of your car, since there is potential for massive recalls in the year 2000. If possible, get the dealer to give you something in writing which guarantees the car is completely compliant. Even so, we recommend you avoid going any distance by car the last night of 1999. If you must go, at least carry an emergency kit and a cell phone. You really don't want to be stranded somewhere on a cold winter night without supplies like a sleeping bag, warm clothes, food, and water. And be very wary of other drivers, since there is a good chance something serious could go wrong in their cars.

Besides the potential problem with embedded chips, you also have to consider the trouble you could have with fuel and the infrastructure. You can't get from here to there if there is no gas in your tank, and the availability of gas might be jeopardized by distribution problems, electrical blackouts shutting down the service stations and cash machines, and the very real possibility of people hoarding gasoline. Start being conscientious about your gas tank. Keep it full all the time. If you establish a constant refilling habit, you should be OK for at least the first few days of 2000.

Highway infrastructure will be very vulnerable to Y2K threats. Computers control bridges and signs, traffic lights and highway lighting, and ventilation systems required in tunnels. Think through your travel. Which places would pose difficulties if there was no power? Route yourself to avoid as many of these obstacles as possible.

Public Transportation

Do you use public transportation such as buses, trains, or ferries? Due to their size and complexity, they are likely to have more microcomputers than your car. The embedded chips in buses and trains will be as vulnerable as the ones found in automobiles, since computers are used for freight car and locomotive scheduling, empty-car distribution, car and train movement, maintenance scheduling, billing, yard classification, inventory control, crew dispatching, work-order management, and interline shipment monitoring. Our advice is to *stay off public transportation the last day of 1999.*

Trains, buses, and ferries rely on computerized scheduling systems to decide departure and arrival times, in addition to the frequency of arrivals and departures. Two buses traveling to the same destination at the same time from opposite directions is not much of a concern, but two trains traveling to the same destination at the same time from opposite directions is terrifying. In the past there was enough human intervention to reduce accidents caused by double scheduling. Now the chances for such wrecks are increased because most of the fail-safe mechanisms are computerized.

Added to the problem and inconvenience of not getting to your destination when expected is the people factor. If something serious occurs, how much panic will there be? Even if Y2K is more irritating than life-threatening, the psychological impact of the situation might cause fear, panic, and looting. Police sources say criminals are already making plans to take advantage of Y2K troubles, so be wary of traveling to your New Year's Eve celebration on a bus, train, or tram.

Air Travel During Y2K

Air travelers are more likely to encounter Y2K troubles than bus and train travelers, because of the industry's reliance on so many computers. Computer systems coordinate cockpit instrument panels, takeoff and landing procedures, collision detection, navigation, and communication with air traffic control. In addition to a plane's roughly 500 computers, each airport air traffic control uses computers, and each airline has computers handling reservations and scheduling. The potential for disaster is enormous.

The FAA air traffic control system is one of the country's biggest and most complicated computer systems, but it is also one of the oldest. The age of the system means it could have Y2K compliance challenges, even though the government announced it would begin replacing the entire system in late 1998. The impact of Y2K on the extremely complex global reservation system could also be tremendous.

Aircraft maintenance and repair is another concern for air travelers. The FAA creates regulations for scheduled checkups and repairs, and carries out appropriate investigations to ensure they are done properly. Aircraft manufacturers also establish guidelines and recommendations for maintenance and replacement of parts, but it is the airlines which actually carry out the maintenance. The real work of creating safe planes is performed by the employees of the airline company, not by the maker or the FAA. Each airline has its own maintenance-scheduling computer system, and each is working to ensure the upkeep of its planes is safe.

Another aspect of scheduling involves the flight crew. If you have much experience flying on commercial airlines, you may know that scheduling is a complex affair. Flights are frequently delayed because the crew was stuck in another city due to bad weather. Imagine the troubles that could ensue if Y2K glitches completely confuse the elaborate computer-generated schedules. Strict regulations prevent the airlines from requiring crews to work additional hours to compensate for scheduling mistakes, so there will be no easy fix if a crew does not show up for its appointed flight.

Airports have a remarkably convoluted infrastructure system and are behind in becoming Y2K compliant. The Air Transport Association surveyed 81 airports in the United States, and found only 20 were on schedule to fix Y2K computer glitches. Nine airports were somewhat behind, 24 were more than three months behind, and the remaining 28 were airports that *had no plan in place for dealing with Y2K*. Consider all the different aspects of employees, travelers, restaurants, bars, shops, and shuttle buses connected to a modern airport. Computers affect all of these elements, and if the power goes out there will be chaos. The best advice: Try to avoid flying the first month of 2000.

Shipping and Handling

In addition to the transportation of people, there is the distribution of goods—the lifeblood of American business. The distribution of commodities will definitely feel the impact of any disruption to transportation. International shipping is at risk because of the expense of repairing Y2K and the lack of programmers available to fix the problems in other parts of the world. Approximately 80,000 transport ships sail the world's waters, and cargo delivery problems or risks of collisions from faulty navigational systems are examples of possible headaches confronting maritime shippers.

Computer automation has invaded the shipping industry so that crews aren't required to have the seaworthy skills of their forefathers. This could pose a hazard at sea if computer systems malfunction and the ship has to be operated solely by the crew. At sea, a small glitch can cause a major problem. The modern commercial vessel is increasingly dependent on technology for such things as navigation, propulsion, communication, and safety controls. On shore, port managers depend on embedded chips to manage cargo, run elevators, and maintain security. There are serious concerns about systems which rely on archived data used in planned maintenance operations and date-stamped alarm systems.

The procedure for fixing the Y2K problem is the same on or offshore. Shippers are finding it necessary to replace entire computer systems—a process that is both costly and time-consuming. Complicating the matter is the lack of cooperation and communication between ship owners and equipment manufacturers. As in many other big businesses, the maritime industry has seen its share of mergers and acquisitions, and the end result is a loss of critical data. Equipment manufacturers are having a hard time assessing equipment for the shipboard Y2K problem. *In a recent study, the U.S. Coast Guard surveyed marine manufacturers and found 20 percent of the embedded chips tested were not Y2K compliant.* This discovery is causing the Coast Guard to consider the possibility of including Y2K compliance as part of a standard safety checklist.

Onshore, the Y2K glitch has freight forwarders worrying about their cargo. Shippers are looking at fines as well as delays if computers fail to accurately handle data transfers to customs officials. Security is a major concern as well, as is the possibility of refrigeration systems turning off, spoiling the cargo. The end result of all these shipping problems could be a lack of products. You might decide to avoid all modes of transit except walking in the year 2000, yet your life could easily be altered by inadequate distribution and transportation troubles.

Making Wise Travel Choices

Once you've realized the potential dilemmas, the next step is to consider your options and initiate preparations. Begin by meeting with your family members and discussing the problems of travel. If you usually attend separate activities on New Year's Eve, suggest you all stay home in 1999, or at least all go to the same events. It's better to be stuck at the same party than to be scattered around the city. Remember, there is a good chance if you get stranded somewhere you're not going to be able to call home because the phones will be down. If there is the possibility of an emergency occurring, it is better to be in a relatively safe environment than at the top of some hotel with 200 frightened people.

Factor into your car travel the infrastructure problems mentioned earlier. If you drive to work, how many intersections with stoplights are there? How many drawbridges? How many tunnels? It might be wise to list all your regular destinations like work, school, sports activities, grocery stores, and the like. Once you've done this for all members of your family, discuss alternative routes and alternative modes of transportation. Could you bicycle to work? Could your kids walk to school or the grocery store? Can you carpool with neighbors or friends? Is the public transportation system operating, and if it is, could you use it? Are there shorter routes using only surface streets? Can you avoid bridges, tunnels, and stoplights?

Having examined your family's dependence on cars, next look at other modes of transportation. Perhaps you and your family live in the inner city and don't own a car. In that case, how will you plan to travel? Do you use public transportation like buses and trains? If so, what will you do if the bus is down for an extended period of time? How will you move around if the subway doesn't work? *Try to discover several different ways of transporting yourselves.* A scooter or motorcycle might be a possible solution, since you could probably store enough gas for a scooter to last quite awhile.

Is it possible to rearrange your life so you don't need to travel much? People who have home-based businesses are in ideal situations, because their need for transportation is minimized. They will still feel the impact of Y2K on shipping and receiving, but at least they won't be out in the confusion of the streets. If your main destination is the workplace, could you move closer to it, so that you might be able to walk to work? If you are married, make sure your partner won't be inconvenienced by the move.

If your work requires plane travel, and airports become chaotic and difficult, find out if trains are an alternative. It's unlikely all means of transportation will collapse at the same time or in the same place, so if one system is temporarily out of order in one part of the country, that doesn't necessarily mean it will be out of order somewhere else. If you must travel a great distance, anticipate trouble and think about alternative modes of transit. Carry a small emergency kit consisting of a change of clothes and some basic toiletries, and be prepared to be patient.

The Two- to Three-Day Plan

January 1, 2000, is a Saturday. Many people could be traveling on this day, or trying to get home for work on Monday. Our suggestion is to avoid long trips that weekend if at all possible. The less distance you travel, the less you are vulnerable to potential problems. If you must travel and are using some mode of public transportation, find out if the company's vehicles are Y2K compliant. If they aren't (or if they don't know) *find another company or consider another mode of transportation.* By the end of 1999, there should be a much greater public awareness of anticipated Y2K trouble. It's very likely businesses will advertise their compliance. Assuming that's the case, pick your transportation company accordingly.

Before the end of the year, find out about the compliance of your car. If you can afford it, consider purchasing a new vehicle or an older one that predates embedded chips. Expect traffic delays caused by such things as traffic-light outages and bridges that are out of commission. Plan carefully for any trip. Even if you have been living in the same area all your life, consult detailed maps and familiarize yourself with alternative routes. Drive very defensively and be aware of problems in other cars on January 1. And keep in mind that you don't know the mental condition of other drivers—Y2K could cause tremendous amounts of road rage due to extreme amounts of fear and frustration.

A three-day emergency could have some affect on the availability of food supplies and other goods because of transportation and distribution problems. If you have followed our earlier advice, you will be prepared for it. We're not suggesting you shut yourself away from the outside world and go nowhere, but we do recommend you carefully consider the need for any trip. Much will depend upon the severity of the situation. If the problems of Y2K are serious, there won't be much movement anyway. People will be too busy trying to survive the outages and other calamities.

The One-Month Plan

A full month of transportation emergencies would be a crippling disaster by itself, without factoring in communication, utility, and banking problems. If your business relies strongly on salespeople being out in the field and they can't get out there, you've got economic problems looming on the horizon. Yet the real impact is likely to be felt because of shipping troubles. Businesses won't be able to get what they need if trains, trucks, planes, and ships cannot get materials and products to them. Conversely, businesses can't move their product if those same modes of transportation are down.

We don't think every vehicle in the world is going to stop running. Older vehicles are immune to problems with computers, though there will be fuel supply problems and highway infrastructure troubles. Many businesses will have their systems compliant in time, but will need to be flexible and consider their alternatives for surviving the pinch on their customer base. If one airline is down, businesses will have to try another airline. If airline travel is impractical, you'll have to consider trains or buses. If your car doesn't work, perhaps the car of a family member or a friend does. *Looking for alternatives is going to be the key to personal and business transportation.*

If communication systems are not affected by Y2K in a major way, you might find your company using such services as teleconferencing and videoconferencing to reduce the amount of travel. Telephones, computers, and all other communication devices were created to cut down on the need for person-to-person meetings, so we should be ready to take full advantage of them.

The One-Year Plan

Severely impaired transportation for a year is possible, but difficult to envision. The impact of such a catastrophe would be felt by the corporate community. Businesses would go bankrupt simply because they couldn't get their goods and services to customers. If your business depends upon your car, you need to anticipate a yearlong disaster and get a vehicle that is fully compliant. You will also need to examine your dependency upon shipping and receiving—for example, a small service-oriented business might not have much reliance on supplies or raw materials. If you discover you are extremely dependent upon transportation, perhaps you might consider changing your business.

If you believe Y2K troubles will stretch for a year, you had better carefully read our suggestions for food, water, and other supplies, because of potential problems with distribution. You might contemplate moving to an area where you are not dependent upon public transportation, or even consider living in your car, camper, or RV. Walking or bicycling might just be the best and most dependable mode of transportation. While it's not easy to change your lifestyle, it might be the key to your survival.

YOUR Y2K PLANNING GUIDE

20 Tips for Surviving Transportation Trouble

1. Avoid traveling long distances from December 31 to January 15.
2. Avoid shorter traveling from December 31 to January 3.
3. Find out if your car is Y2K compliant.
4. Explore what aspects of your local highway infrastructure might be affected.
5. Be aware of problems with other drivers and other cars.
6. Keep your gas tank full.
7. If you use public transportation, find out which companies and vehicles are compliant.
8. Be certain you have enough food, water, and other necessary supplies.
9. Talk with your family about potential problems.
10. Find alternative ways of travel.
11. Limit your amount of travel.
12. List your "most-traveled-to" destinations and find alternative routes.
13. Have a family meeting to discuss transportation questions.
14. Carry a small emergency kit with you on trips, and be prepared for problems.
15. Keep an emergency kit in your car, in case you become stranded.
16. Realize the potential impact on business and make plans accordingly.
17. If possible, use technological devices like videoconferencing to cut down on traveling.
18. Consider moving closer to work.
19. Consider moving to another area where you will be less dependent upon transportation.
20. Buy a bike or motor scooter and keep it maintained.

THIRTEEN

Money Madness

Larry Burkett, founder of Christian Financial Concepts, started his November 1998 letter to those on his mailing list with these words: "We're on a 14-month countdown to the year 2000." He goes on to list Y2K as one of the problems that suggests difficult days may lie ahead. As a recognized leader of an investment and accounting firm, Burkett is careful to not say anything which could be construed as causing panic. At the same time, he makes it clear the potential problems due to Y2K and related computer noncompliance should lead us to prepare for the future. We aren't bankers or financial advisers, and we highly encourage you to speak with a financial adviser before making important financial decisions, but we think everyone should take stock of their financial situation before January 1, 2000.

No one is quite sure what will happen to the banking system if Y2K disrupts the service and corrupts its records. Last year congressman James Leach quoted Federal Reserve Chief Alan Greenspan as saying, "Ninety-nine percent readiness for the year 2000 will not be enough. It must be 100 percent. Thus, the message seems clear: All financial institutions

What's Ahead

- **Y2K and Your Bank**
- **The Problem of Size**
- **The Domino Theory**
- **The Two-to Three-Day Plan**
- **The One-Month Plan**
- **The One-Year Plan**
- **Your Y2K Planning Guide**

must be ready: . . . agencies . . . service providers . . . vendors . . . bank customers . . . and international counter parties must be ready." Unfortunately, most are not ready.

Y2K and Your Bank

Banks function on the basis of what is called fractional reserve banking. They only need to keep a fraction of their reserves on hand to meet the day-to-day demands of customers doing cash withdrawals. The underlying fact behind this practice is that a large reserve of money is not present in banks. When the average person deposits 1000 dollars into his account, the entire 1000 dollars is sent to the Federal Reserve. The bank now has a credit reserve of 1000 dollars, and it will begin to loan that money out to others who need it. The loans made by the bank are both an asset and a liability. It doesn't have the cash on hand, but it is owed to the bank in good faith by a borrower, therefore the bank can show its books remain balanced. In conjunction with the banks, the Federal Reserve system uses this process to "create money" by arranging for local banks to have money to loan.

When you deposit your paycheck, a computer debits your employer's account and credits yours. When you write a check to the utility company, the same thing happens. Credits and debits flow back and forth within the banking system, but nothing ever really leaves it. Over 90 percent of our money is handled through computer entries, and at a rate of five dollars per dollar of deposits, the Federal Reserve makes sure the money has been lent out to depositors. This system works fine as long as the money never leaves the system. Unfortunately, there are inherent dangers in this system.

If a power outage shuts down computers and businesses, people will require cash in order to purchase food, water, and fuel. They could all head to the banks at once, creating a "run" on cash reserves. When demands exceed the bank's ability to pay, it forces the calling in of loans, adding further pressure to the local economy. Those whose notes are called will need cash to pay—exactly the thing the bank doesn't have. This scenario can lead to the possible closing of the bank. On top of this, recognize that banks loan money to each other, so when one bank fails, other banks will be affected, whether they are Y2K compliant or not. And they all rely on electronic records, which could be either lost or corrupted from problems with computer records that are not Y2K compliant. The scenario is clear: *Y2K has the potential to trigger an economic collapse.*

If businesses have problems dealing with the banking system, they will revert to cash, not computer transactions. Customers wanting goods or services will go to the bank demanding cash and won't be able to get any. Your local banker will tell you your deposit is guaranteed by the FDIC, so the government can assure you the money will be there when you need it. But that's not necessarily the case. Only one or two percent of the deposits in the banking system could be covered if all were called in at the same time.

Historians tell us that "confidence" is what holds our banking system together, and it was a loss of confidence more than any other factor which created so many troubles for banks at the advent of the Great Depression. When people begin to see runs on banks, foreclosed loans, and an inability to produce hard cash, their confidence in the system drops. That is followed by an increase in bad debt from businesses that are unable to get or raise money and repay their loans. And while the FDIC claims to insure your deposits, if the losses are in the billions, they will simply not have enough cash to monetize the debt.

On top of these problems, there is the strong possibility of a rise in security problems as a result of hackers taking advantage of Y2K disruptions. Banks are already aware that elements within organized crime are trying to find ways to use Y2K to their advantage. The delicate problem regarding sensitive data such as customers' personal records is also a concern. The destruction or corruption of transaction records is a serious problem, as are miscalculated savings, checking, and brokerage account transactions. Following January 1, there will doubtless be increased litigation over lost records and information, further straining the bank's ability to cope.

The Problem of Size

The Federal Reserve system is the nation's central bank, and without question the largest bank in the world. Every major country depends on the integrity of America's central bank. It moves 1 trillion dollars a day to various customers, and its electronic transfer system serves almost 12,000 major client banks and institutions. Twenty-seven million transfers entered this system in 1995 alone. Experts agree that a mere ten percent error factor could cause untold complications in the world's banking systems—*yet the Fed's computer programs are not Y2K compliant.*

Only 40 percent of our bankers know what the impact of Y2K will be on their bank. Many have approached the problem far too late to actually accomplish any significant changes. And the costs are prohibitive. Chase Manhattan Bank has 336 billion dollars in assets and handles more than a trillion dollars a day. Yet it has 200 million lines of code, running in 15,000 applications, on more than 60,000 desktops, 400 mid-range computers, and multiple mainframes. The company started working on the Y2K problem in 1995. It estimates it will take 800 programmers, at a cost of over 200 million dollars, to fix the problem. A fair question to ask anyone preparing for Y2K is, "Do you have a backup plan?" The answer to that question, as far as most banks are concerned, is "No."

Credit-card companies such as Visa and Master Card have had to deal with the sticky issue of Y2K-compliant expiration dates. The problem is so massive and poses such a risk that these two companies are actually exchanging information. With over 13 million point-of-sale terminals to process purchase approvals—some of which may not be compliant—the "00" expiration has already been causing systems to lock up and cardholders to be denied credit. Consider the number of vendors, service providers, and other partners in this huge business, and you can see the magnitude of the problem.

It takes time to test and retest fixes. If financial institutions and their computer-interdependent partners haven't started the fixing soon enough, there is no way the project can be completed before January 1, 2000. Worst of all, other countries are further behind in their compliancy than the United States. The Euro conversion, costing 100 billion dollars worldwide, has bankers in Europe ignoring the Y2K problem. Japan poses the biggest threat to the American economy because it is so heavily invested in U.S. markets, and most Japanese banks are just beginning to tackle the problem. Many banks in Latin America and Asia are still further behind. It could take only five percent of the world bank's payment systems to fail to create a global liquidity crisis.

The Domino Theory

You have probably seen someone set up a long row of dominoes, perhaps taking hours to arrange an elaborate system of mazes and turns. When that first domino is gently pushed, it sets into motion a force that, correctly arranged, causes every domino to fall in order. The fear among some banking experts is that a domino theory will attack the banks and financial institutions of the world on January 1, 2000.

In real time the dominoes would fall like this: If banks close, goods and services deliveries will stop because the merchant who needs the supplies cannot write a check for the delivery. Paying in cash will not be an option because banks will not let businesses or shoppers get extra cash before they close down. Shelves in stores will be empty because trucks will not be able to make their deliveries. With nothing moving and products not selling, businesses will start to fold. Loans will go unpaid, further adding to the crisis. In the span of a few months, the entire economy is in tatters.

Are we predicting this scenario? No. We believe there are some checks and balances, and that the good faith of the

American people will withstand some isolated problems. But Y2K could cause serious financial struggles around the globe, and once the world economy is in decline, it becomes hard to reverse.

Wall Street and securities industries depend heavily on computers. In pre-Depression days, the volume of shares per day topped out at five million, backlogs were common, and employees worked overtime to record the trades. Today the daily volume on the stock market can exceed *500 million shares per day*—and they are all done by computers. Date-sensitive computers, the massive volume of transactions, limited programming resources, and the short time left all contribute to the possibility of a serious stock-market tumble. As word gets out among investors about Y2K—especially the amount of money needed to fix the problem and the imminent ticking clock—the market will start to wane.

Realistically, Y2K could cause massive problems through a domino effect. We all depend on the computer, so our lives will certainly continue, but planning ahead for a possible financial crisis would be wise. Personal debt in America has long been a parasite eating away at our economy. Too many people have financed their purchasing through credit cards, so that they feel trapped by their debt. Almost daily, homeowners get calls from finance companies wanting to refinance their home and loan them the equity. Credit-card companies send line-of-credit checks that can be written whenever needed, preapproved and with no waiting. Anyone over 18 years of age can get a preapproved credit card with thousands of dollars of what seems to be "free money." Cars, often grander than we may need, are easily financed, as are vacations, appliances, and home furnishings. The result is a huge debt owed to banks—debt that might not be easily paid back in case of an economic depression, leading to numerous business and bank failures.

Our response needs to be to reclaim our financial independence. The most important thing you can do is sit down today and make a plan to become debt-free. Pay off your credit cards and stop borrowing against your future. For some people, selling property, downgrading cars, and saving more money is going to be crucial to get through the year 2000.

The Two- to Three-Day Plan

If you think your bank is going to be closed for a few days, the solution is simple: *Get some extra cash out of the bank.* Don't wait until the last minute. We recommend you take out adequate cash by October, in case your bank is caught in a "cash crunch." Of course, your favorite grocery stores might also be closed for a few days, so stock up on some of your favorite foods and wait out the storm.

We also recommend you lead your family in a discussion about money and finance. Take the fake money from a Monopoly board game and deal it onto your kitchen table, equal to the amount you make in a year. Then show everyone your budget, adding up costs for things like rent, utilities, food, and your current monthly obligations. Start making piles of play money, representing what you pay out. After everything has been paid, what's left over is the family spending money. Help your kids see the importance of using money wisely, and look for small things you can do to make a big difference in your finances.

The One-Month Plan

If you believe Y2K will generate a longer breakdown of goods and services and has the potential to seriously impact our nation's economy, you had better sit down and think through how you'll handle a cash crunch. *Plan to have adequate money out of the bank and into your hands by late 1999.* Try to determine what sort of financial drain Y2K could have on your money, and come up with some ideas for saving extra money. Ask your family members what they could do to limit extra spending, and make sure to have your monthly payments in order and manageable. If you can, prepay them for the first two months of the year 2000 and get receipts. Consider having a garage sale this summer in order to get rid of some stuff and raise extra capital.

Begin to make hard copies of all your financial assets, deeds, wills, stocks and bonds, and the title to your house and car. You may want to invest in gold coins, since it is a medium of exchange which has proven valuable for centuries. In a total economic meltdown, American greenbacks may not retain their value, but gold will probably still be of great value.

The One-Year Plan

It is hard to imagine the American economy completely collapsing, but if Y2K were to persist for a year, the damage to consumers and small businesses would be incalculable. Banks would be without money, homes would be foreclosed, jobs would be lost, and in a very short time people would be forced to create a new life. Optimism would give way to reality after several months of discomfort, and it is doubtful the government will have any easy solutions. Therefore, if you believe Y2K is going to be a serious problem, a long-term financial plan is critical.

Have an adequate supply of cash on hand, and invest some of your money into buying gold coins. *If at all possible, you want to be debt-free, so that you are unencumbered by banks and financial institutions.* Assuming you have created a cache of food supplies, your best option will be to create a life where your family can be self-sufficient. For the modern American family, that will require some significant sacrifices. Again, consider where you will be living and whom you will be close to. When the Indonesian economy collapsed last year, there were riots in the streets.

Protecting your family and possessions will be key. Savings accounts may be wiped out and pension moneys may not be available. Governmental checks will be slow, if they arrive at all, so think through a budget carefully. How much would your family need to survive for a year?

Finally, we encourage you to talk openly with your mate about the possible changes wrought by Y2K. Money troubles are one of the biggest dangers to a marriage, and if this scenario takes place there will be many families facing difficult financial times. Talk through the issues of change and lifestyles so that you both are prepared in case you should need to make significant alterations for your family. Preparing for a long-term economic crisis means having to talk about some hard subjects, but if you don't talk, you won't feel prepared.

YOUR Y2K PLANNING GUIDE

15 Questions to Ask Yourself Before the Year 2000

1. How much money do I make?
2. Where does it go?
3. Do we have a realistic, workable budget?
4. How much can we set aside to prepare for Y2K?
5. How much could I spend right now to purchase the things we'll need?
6. What could we sell to help raise more money?
7. Do I have copies of all my accounts, titles, insurance policies, stocks, and other financial investments?
8. How much cash on hand will we want on January 1, 2000?
9. Can we prepay some of our monthly obligations?
10. Do we have hard-copy receipts of our major payments?
11. Do we have hard-copy records of our home and car ownership?
12. Should we purchase gold coins as a hedge against financial collapse?
13. How can we decrease our debt?
14. How could we become debt-free?
15. What lifestyle changes will we expect to make as a family?

PART FOUR

OBSTACLE
AND OPPORTUNITY

FOURTEEN

The Prolonged Emergency

The most overwhelming thing about Y2K is how it affects so many different aspects of our lives. We've tried to show you some of these aspects and give you some ways to prepare because we firmly believe the better prepared you are for a crisis, the better your chances of survival. Therefore, examine your beliefs about the potential severity and length of the Y2K emergency and prepare for that degree of danger. If you think it will last a few days, plan for that possibility. If you think it could last for a year or longer, make appropriate plans with that scenario in mind.

Be certain you have the essential ingredients for survival: food and water. Consider the impact of electrical outages on your heating and lighting. Realize the need for medical emergency supplies and know basic treatments for the most common injuries and illnesses. Understand the need for safety practices and the importance of knowing how to defend yourself and your family. Prepare for communication and transportation problems. If you have done all of these things, you should feel ready.

What's Ahead

- **Flexible, Mobile, and Liquid**
- **Shutting Off Utilities**
- **Your Computer**
- **If It All Falls Apart**
- **Yes, You Can**
- **Your Y2K Planning Guide**

The amount of change in your life after January 1, 2000, will depend on the extent of damage caused by Y2K. Three days without your regular comforts might make you unhappy, but won't disrupt your lifestyle. A month would be much more traumatic, possibly causing you to change the way your family lives. A year would certainly have long-lasting ramifications affecting our culture and the way we live our lives.

At some point during your preparation, you need to sit down with your family and discuss the potential change to your family's lifestyle after January 1, 2000. Anticipating this transformation emotionally and intellectually will make the situation easier to handle and keep you from avoiding the reality of the change. The very fact you are asking your family to help prepare for a possible emergency alerts them to the possibility of major changes. Openly discussing the future will help make those changes easier to handle when they actually occur. The more extreme your preparation, the more intense your discussion about the future should be. Everyone in your family needs to know how severe you think the situation might be and what that means for them.

Flexible, Mobile, and Liquid

If you're worried about the possibility of severe Y2K disruptions, consider the three most important criteria for survival: flexibility, mobility, and liquidity. *The ability to adapt to whatever situation confronts you is a necessity for personal survival.* Rigidity and old thinking can be lethal, while being flexible can keep you alive. The less fixed your living conditions, the better. A rented apartment can be left behind, if necessary. The more quickly you can move your family and important possessions, the better-equipped you are for survival. The liquidity of your financial condition is crucial for survival. Wasting precious time trying to get your nonliquid assets converted to cash will hurt your survival chances. You may not feel it necessary to take such precautions, but knowing you can if it becomes necessary at least helps you become prepared.

We would like to think the actions by corporate executives, computer experts, and government leaders during the remaining days of 1999 will save us from Y2K disaster, but we contend it's better to be overly cautious and take appropriate measures than to simply trust the actions of others and do nothing. In this section we're going to explore the importance of anticipating an emergency while keeping flexibility in mind.

These days most Americans don't usually anticipate a crisis. Our culture believes in happy endings. We just assume nothing bad will ever happen, and we rarely take any kind of action to prepare. But we know a Y2K crisis is coming, whether you believe it will be large or small, so each of us has plenty of warning. And the very act of planning by storing supplies and practicing preventive maintenance will prove beneficial for any kind of emergency. The food and water you've stored for the Y2K disaster can be used for an earthquake, blackout, or hurricane.

Think through the things that are important to you: If you had to leave, what would you take? How would you move, particularly if your vehicles don't work or you know all traffic signals and lights are out? How much cash do you feel you'll need to have on hand? And if American currency is struck hard by inflation, what alternative means of barter could you use? Having a plan in place, being flexible, and having some form of exchange with you are important aspects of being prepared for Y2K.

Shutting Off Utilities

One thing you will want to consider as you prepare for Y2K is *shutting off your utilities*. If there is a blackout or brownout, you will want to turn off your electricity in order to protect your home from power surges. We also suggest you consider turning off your gas and water, simply because of the domino effect—if your electricity goes out, more than likely the other two will also fail because the pumps working them will no longer function. Here are some general guidelines for shutting off your utilities;

however, we strongly encourage you to talk with a plumber, electrician, and utility representative before taking any action yourself. Find out what an expert has to say about your home before attempting to handle potentially dangerous situations.

Electricity is the most crucial. A huge surge in your power could cause many problems to your wiring, your appliances, and your computers. The major electrical service box in your home is called a panel or fuse box. Know where your service box is, how to access it, and how to turn off the power. Most homes have a flat rectangular box on the wall with a meter, often with a round glass dome above it. Open the lid to the service box, and you'll find a whole row of switches known as circuit breakers. Find the first of these switches and you'll see two of them joined together with a metal connector. This is the main switch, and the one you need in order to shut off your power. Grasp the two coupled switches with your thumb and fore-finger—they will be pointing left—and push them to the right until they click. The switch might be quite stiff, but a firm push will move it to the right, thus breaking the circuit and pro-tecting your home. (Once power is restored to your neighbor-hood, simply reverse this procedure, pushing the main switch to the left and returning power to your home.)

If the above description doesn't fit your situation, you'll need to contact your electric company and find out what pro-cedure you'll need to follow. Older homes might have a fuse box, which will require you to pull fuse cartridges out. Remember that shutting off all power will mean you'll need to reset all clocks and timers after your electricity is restored.

Gas is the next important utility. If your furnace has an elec-tric pilot light and you lose electricity, your furnace will no longer work (though if you have an older gas furnace or hot water heater with a permanent pilot light, it will remain burning as long as there is gas in the line). The problem associ-ated with Y2K is that no one knows if the utility companies will be able to control the pumping of gas. A gas surge in the lines, particularly into a home in which the pilot lights have gone out, could lead to an explosive situation.

If you decide to shut off your gas line, simply locate your gas meter—usually found near the ground by a wall close to the front of your house. There will be a pipe coming out of the ground going into the meter, a large round pressure regulator with pipes coming in and out of it, and a block of metal sticking out like a flat short bar. That is the gas shutoff valve, and we'll tell you right now it is difficult to turn off. Familiarize yourself with its location and learn how to turn the valve using a large crescent wrench. You might want to practice this once or twice, since a small turn of this valve won't shut off the gas to your home. In a practice session, don't actually shut off your gas; simply go through the procedure so that you know what to do.

If you can't get any movement at all from your gas shutoff valve—which isn't uncommon, since nobody ever turns them—you will want to contact your gas company and let them know your gas shutoff valve needs fixing. In a real emergency, a working valve might be the difference between safety and an explosion.

The last utility, and the one with the least potential danger, is your water. It's a good idea to shut it off and avoid potential damage to your pipes, but it isn't absolutely necessary. You probably have a main water meter located near the street, on the ground in front of your house. Search for a concrete or metal lid to a box—the lid usually has a slot rather than a handle. Under the lid is the water shutoff valve.

You may need a screwdriver or crow bar to create leverage to lift the lid. Inside you'll notice the water meter and a big pipe running across the box. Directly above the meter is either a large metal handle or a metal bar similar to your gas shutoff valve. You shut off the water by turning that valve or pulling the handle down. You may be able to use the same crescent wrench you used for shutting off the gas, or you may need to get more leverage by placing a long bar over the handle and giving it a yank. Newer neighborhoods might have a long stem or shutoff key. Much like turning off the gas, a lot of strength and patience will be required to shut off your water valve.

Never hesitate to call the service companies if you can't discover the answers yourself or if you have any troubles with the procedures.

Your Computer

How will Y2K affect your personal computer? It depends on how you use it and how old your system is. It's quite possible your PC is completely Y2K compliant and on January 1 nothing will happen. Even if something does happen, it might not matter if you only use your PC for electronic games and occasional home projects. But if you use your PC to network to your office or run a home-based business, you should take extra precautions. Your word-processing programs, data base, and accounting programs will need to be made Y2K compliant or you run the risk of losing all your information.

Hardware is susceptible mainly because it keeps track of time. Almost all home PCs have an internal clock. In older computers the clock and the logic that runs it are not Y2K compliant, so even though the display will read "01-01-00," the date may be interpreted as 1900, eventually causing serious trouble with your operating system and software programs. PC-based computers manufactured before 1997 are most vulnerable, but even some of the ones made during 1997 are susceptible. Apple Macintosh systems seem to be Y2K compliant. Talk to a computer technician before attempting to make changes and to find more complete information.

The standard way to test your PC clock is to manually reset the system clock to 11:59 P.M. on December 31, 1999, then wait a few minutes and see what happens. However, *before you try this make sure you have backups of all your important files*. If the computer crashes, you want to be able to get your work back. If the test appears to work, repeat the experiment, this time turning your computer off after you've set the clock, waiting a few minutes, and turning it back on again. Fortunately, if you detect a hardware problem you may be able to get a replacement for little or no cost from your local computer dealer.

The next area of concern is your operating system. Most of the older versions of MS-DOS and MS Windows are not compliant, so they will revert to January 4, 1980—the date of their initial design. More current systems such as Windows NT, Windows 98, and Apple's MacOS are fully Y2K compliant. If your home PC is a relatively new Pentium-based computer or a MacPower PC, you're probably OK. But if you are still running an old 286 or 386 class Intel computer and you've got DOS or Windows 3.1, you've got trouble. Most of that trouble will exist not in the hardware or the operating system, but in the software programs. Some programs may not be date-sensitive, but if any of the programs you deem absolutely essential to your home or business survival are not compliant, make it a priority to find a remedy. Word processing, accounting programs, and data-base programs are the most likely to be date-sensitive.

Since Y2K is a universal problem, the remedies for software glitches can usually be had for no cost. The easiest way to get these solutions is from the vendor's Internet site, but you should be able to call the vendor's customer service department for assistance. If you have any really old versions, you probably won't be able to find a free update. The vendor will suggest you upgrade to the latest edition—and they will charge you for it. And there might be additional costs if you need to acquire extra memory for your hard drive.

Obviously, old software made by small companies now out of business will need to be replaced, and most applications you've created yourself might have problems. If you stored date-related information with a two-digit year, you should count on it fouling up your computer.

If It All Falls Apart

So far we've only contemplated the crisis lasting a year. Even a year seems like a long time and may appear extremely unlikely. However, if you really think about all the interconnected elements and how one thing can affect another—an electrical blackout affects telecommunication, and that outage disrupts transportation, which in turn disrupts business, and so on—you begin to realize the potential for a decade-long global disaster. It has happened before—in 1929. The depression lasted until 1939, and some economists will tell you the Great Depression did not really come to an end until the war broke out in 1941. That time, the federal government came to the rescue and instituted programs to help save America. This time, the government itself might be jeopardized.

There are speculations the Internal Revenue Service will implode because of all the computer problems. There are worries the same thing will happen to Social Security and Medicare. These are wild guesses perhaps, but they are based on the evidence that 71 percent of the federal government's mission-critical systems are not Y2K compliant and must be replaced or repaired. The time and money needed to fix these problems is running out.

If businesses collapse, if local and federal governments collapse, what happens to us? What happens to our society and civilization? How would life be different for your family if America as we know it ceased to exist?

Yes, You Can

We seem to forget that humanity and culture have evolved over thousands of years. Modern American culture grew out of the industrial age, when each person pulled his own weight, and survival was generally a daily concern. We have always survived and evolved because of our minds. Primitive man learned to make fires and wheels. He explored, invented, and progressed. Modern man has created an information age, in which technology and science have moved us into never-before-dreamed areas of creativity. Yet that same technology which brought us information on a grand scale might move us back to a simpler, harder style of life.

Human intelligence and human spirit are truly wonderful gifts. We each have the innate ability to solve problems and better ourselves. We have seen plagues, famine, natural disasters, and world wars, and we survived. For that reason, we believe in American ingenuity and the can-do spirit of our people to get through the problems caused by Y2K. Even if we face a prolonged emergency, with troubles continuing for several years, we'll get through it. Our faith in God will help us. In this last section of our book, we will explore how we can face the coming obstacles and overcome them. The future might look a bit bleak, but we have the ability to not only survive . . . we can flourish. We have done it before. We can do it again.

YOUR Y2K PLANNING GUIDE

Ten Steps to Consider in a Prolonged Emergency

1. Make sure you have the supplies you need for a prolonged emergency.
2. Talk with your family about the lifestyle changes you might make.
3. Consider what you can do to maintain a healthy emotional state.
4. Ask yourself, "Is our family plan flexible?"
5. Think through your options. What will you do if you need to make changes to your plans?
6. Consider your mobility. Make sure you can leave if you need to.
7. Maintain your liquidity. Have enough money on hand for the situation.
8. Know how to shut off all your utilities.
9. Check your personal computer and make sure it is Y2K compatible.
10. If you are married, talk through your plans with your mate. Make sure you are in agreement with the choices you've made.

FIFTEEN

Keeping Your Job

The saying goes that recession is when your neighbor is out of work, depression is when you are out of work. Y2K is like a large, poisonous snake that has been hiding for several years. It is moving now, slowly, behind the scenes, shielded from the majority of Americans' eyes. Soon it will begin to shake its tail violently, warning of a coming strike. Your company may be one of those wounded by its bite. Big and powerful forces will help shape what happens to jobs and businesses in this country, but the only sure way to avoid the danger is to make careful preparations.

It's possible your company will be shaken by Y2K. Will it be able to stay in business? If you were asked to go without pay for a month, would you stay at your job or look for something else? Unfortunately, chances are high many hardworking, self-sacrificing Americans will find themselves victims of unemployment. Do you have a plan in place if you were to lose your job? Your livelihood, your lifestyle, and your family's welfare might be shaken. Make sure you take steps to survive as a family.

What's Ahead

- **Chicken Little**
- **What About Your Office?**
- **Saving and Maintaining Income**
- **If the Economy Falters**
- **The Two- to Three-Day Plan**
- **The One-Month Plan**
- **The One-Year Plan**
- **Your Y2K Planning Guide**

Chicken Little

Americans are slow to grasp potential threats Y2K will bring to their lifestyles. One writer has predicted most Americans will not become aware of the danger of Y2K until the fall of 1999, when computer glitches begin to negatively influence records, credit cards, banks, and the stock market. However, he went on to predict that even when faced with serious problems, *the majority of people will choose to do nothing.* They want to believe we are like Chicken Little, yelling about the sky falling. Though they could be facing a cold, dark winter with decreasing amounts of food and increasing amounts of crime and disease, they choose to ignore the warnings. It will only be the days after, when businesses begin to fail and mission-critical systems no longer work, that most people will take notice of Y2K.

Unless we are prepared for disruption, we will be victims. Many people want to believe America can overcome the crisis, but they refuse to accept it will become a major disaster. A recent survey showed that two out of three businesses did not have a plan to deal with Y2K as of December 1998. The Gallup organization claims 75 percent of small businesses have done nothing to prepare. Insurance companies are concluding they cannot and will not cover Y2K-related failures—they will be too massive to fulfill. Some experts are predicting seven out of ten Americans will lose their jobs or their present level of income by April 2000. Five of those seven will be on their own, while the others may find work in clerical or agricultural-related services. There will be no unemployment payments or benefits from the government. If the power crisis lasts for a long time, the unemployment rate could rise higher than 55 percent.

This is no Chicken Little story. History reveals Americans have survived in spite of hard times. The Great Depression brought unemployment rates of more than 30 percent, and homelessness became a way of life. It wrought terrible lifestyle changes for families. And while the government arranged workfare programs to help unemployed workers, there were no widespread power outages nor shortages of clean water. Martial law was not widely imposed to restore order, nor did the president grant authority to the government to confiscate forms of energy. Y2K simply offers an obstacle our country has never faced before. The unemployment could be greater, the danger of government control will be stronger, and the attitude of people could be sour.

As federal funding disappears, local governments will have to bear the burden and will run out of funds due to a lack of the means to obtain taxes. Public schooling simply may not be available. Rural populations would struggle with urban refugees flooding into their areas. Food-supply shortages could cause National Guardsmen to go home to meet their own family's needs, resulting in a vacuum of local security. Two groups have an opportunity to emerge in power: organized crime and organized religion.

And though we would like to think business and government will remain strong and revert to manually recording and completing things, the truth is that most businesses, industries, and governments are entirely computer-dependent. They absolutely can't go back to doing their jobs manually. If things really became this bad, would you still be working at your job?

What About Your Office?

Any business that is highly dependent on computer systems may be vulnerable to serious problems. If noncompliant computers control the electronic locks, lights, phone systems, and manufacturing equipment, it may not be possible for employees to function at all. Essential functions such as entering orders, scheduling the activities of people, and managing equipment would have to be completely re-created. If distributors, wholesalers, and independent sales agents cannot conduct business as usual, businesses cannot sell their products, and the companies will go under. *Every business exists mainly to do one thing: make money.* History shows us that businesses failing to make money disappear quickly.

So think about the Y2K problem at your own place of employ. What steps has your company taken to prepare for Y2K? How many programmers within the organization are working on the problem? How large is the "portfolio" of computer systems, and how much of it has already been made Y2K compliant? Are there servers on computers that will not be ready? Which ones are they, and how will they impact the company's operations if they fail? Are the "end-user" programs at your office (that is, the desktop data bases and software programs you use regularly) Y2K compliant? How many of the companies with whom you do business are Y2K compliant? What are the chances of survival if your three top customers go bankrupt? How long could the company survive without line-of-credit loans or other bank-related funding? How long would it take to find a replacement of raw materials suppliers? Is there an alternative plan if things get really bad?

Let's pretend your boss calls you at home early in January and suggests you not come in. Would you continue working, even if you weren't sure of getting paid? Would you be able to live for a month without an income? It isn't hard to imagine several days where you might have to stay home from work in the first few days of the year 2000. Most of us would welcome the break, if it weren't for the impending possibility that our jobs may be cut off in the near future.

Benevolent employers may treat this as a simple crisis and continue providing a salary to their employees, so check with your boss to see if your company plans to pay for missed workdays due to natural disasters. If not, ask if you can use sick or vacation days to avoid loss of pay. If a crisis occurs and you are required to report for work, negotiate the amount of time you could take off without penalty. You may be able to work different hours, shorter hours, or even fewer days.

As we've already suggested, plan for alternative ways of getting to and from work. Figure on traffic jams, road rage, car problems, no car pools, and the need to be able to communicate with your family. Take your cellular phone with you, just in case.

Saving and Maintaining Income

If you don't have long-term money set aside, start a savings plan today. Americans have not traditionally been known as savers, but saving money while you can is your only option. Low interest rates on loans, high interest on savings, and a sky-high stock market all add up to consumer confidence in the U.S. economy, but if unemployment begins to rise, that confidence will be gone. But by setting some money aside, you can prepare yourself and your family for the future.

According to 1993 U.S. Census Bureau data, 11 percent of all American households had zero or negative net worth, and 14 percent had a net worth between 1 dollar and 5000 dollars. That means *if income were to be lost for one month, 25 percent of all American households would be facing serious financial problems.* Perhaps even more scary, only 19 percent of "nuclear family" households have a net worth of 5000 dollars or more. In other words, most young families have not saved anything due to monthly mortgage demands, they have often borrowed money for down payments, they frequently have credit-card debt, and they will find it practically impossible to live more than a couple weeks without an income. If Y2K hits them hard, these families are in serious trouble.

To make matters worse, young people and senior citizens have the highest risk in the face of Y2K. Younger workers have the least amount of savings, and older members of society are near the end of their earning cycle. They are also least flexible when it comes to being ready for a new job, and retirees living on pension checks could be completely devastated. Those who don't have enough savings to last for an extended period of unemployment will deplete their savings and be forced to rely on other sources of income . . . if they can find another source. Even those in their prime working years may have to withdraw a portion of their mutual fund investments or withdraw from their 401k retirement plans. Since they would be withdrawing from long-term savings, they would also not be contributing into those funds, which would likely cause another drop in the stock market. Middle-class investors will feel poorer and will cut back on their spending, and the decrease in consumption demands will eventually cause companies to cut back on production and likely lay off employees.

The higher the unemployment rate, the higher the correlation with the average number of weeks spent unemployed because jobs are harder to find and people remain unemployed longer. Current levels of unemployment vary, but we have kept the unemployment figure around five percent for several years. If this were to double, the average worker could be out of a job for over four months. On top of that, if unemployment doubled, tax revenues would be about 60 percent lower—roughly 24 billion dollars less every month, causing massive government shutdowns or cutbacks in programs and services.

In 1996, General Motors waded through two strikes, one in Canada and the other in the United States. All told, GM lost over 1 billion dollars in profits. Workers in Canada were off for only 20 days due to the strike, but the effect on the national economy was profound. The ripple of a Y2K disruption would be even worse. Business after business will struggle, either trying to do business with others or attempting to solve its own Y2K problem.

Government revenues will also be in crisis, as people out of work cannot pay taxes. Bankrupt businesses do not pay taxes either, and the government doesn't work without tax money. In recent years we have heard about the government running out of money and having to shut down in September or October. This could be a reality under the effects of Y2K.

If the Economy Falters

What would you do if you were without income for a year? Your short-term savings would be gone, having been used for necessities. Excessive spending would be out—there would be no eating out, no vacations, and no new major purchases. Your credit cards would probably have been cut up a long time ago. So what would you do?

Some Americans already live with long-term unemployment. The welfare class, the terminally unemployable, and the handicapped tell personal, true stories of making it through hard times. The fact is, a majority of the American working class have been blessed far beyond their thankfulness. Many may not have to change careers due to Y2K, but it is possible they could spend at least a few days or weeks without employment.

The fact is, January 1, 2000, may not be the end of the economy, but *your company could shut down unexpectedly*. When was the last time you had to look for another job? It may have been years ago. How would you handle a career change? Do you know another field you could easily move into without extensive training or reeducating? Now is the time to look at your industry. You may decide to change now instead of waiting for a layoff. Computer jobs will be in demand for several years into the next century. Organizations will be in great need of programmers, systems analysts, data base designers, and networking and telecommunication experts.

What if the industry you have worked in your entire adult life all of a sudden disappeared? Could you easily make the change? Government-related jobs, when dismantled, affect people in private industry who have built careers around such activities. If the government cuts back drastically on its spending, a recession is sure to follow. A change in the fashion, taste, or mood of society could force certain careers or professions to shut down. Therefore, one strong quality that will be needed for the long haul is flexibility. Look for and be willing to try new and different jobs for short periods of time. Start exploring your gifts and abilities, so you have an idea of what you could do if things turn bad in your industry. And be prepared for changes—often the emotional trauma of being out of work is the toughest adjustment.

The Two- to Three-Day Plan

If Y2K is short-lived, there will be little special planning necessary. However, we suggest you know ahead of time your options within your company. Take a look at your spending habits and deal with personal indebtedness such as credit cards and lines of credit. Above all, start a savings plan so you have a cushion for dealing with the lingering difficulties of Y2K.

The One-Month Plan

If you think the difficulties of Y2K could stretch on for a month, you might as well admit it's going to have some sort of impact on your business. Whether long- or short-term, any computer problem of such magnitude is bound to heavily influence jobs. With that in mind, we encourage you to gather with a network of like-minded people—neighbors, friends, and coworkers who will be supportive, encouraging, and willing to help with basic needs in an emergency. Support, both physical and emotional, will be the key to surviving a career upheaval.

If at all possible, try to ensure you have ample supplies at home so large sums of money aren't needed to survive. And watch closely your financial records and reports, making sure any errors are dealt with immediately. Make sure not to miss your monthly required payments. Keeping your mortgage, car payments, and insurance up-to-date will give you peace of mind as you head into the crisis.

Remember, most of us have never had a forced vacation and will find it very hard to deal with emotionally. Have a plan ready to help with the adjustment of not going to work daily. Get exercise, get out of the house, visit those in need, and do something meaningful to contribute to good mental health.

It would also be wise to update your resumé, printing some copies and having them on hand in case you decide to pursue a new line of work.

The One-Year Plan

If you believe Y2K will last for a year, you might as well admit that most of us will be out of work. Not only will your job be gone, most jobs will be gone. The world could be in a state of economic collapse. If that's the case, make plans now. Invest in some medium of exchange—some experts have suggested gold, wheat, or even ammunition. Make long-term money arrangements.

Get your resumé prepared for immediate use, and plan to look for a job working with your hands. Place all your important personal papers in safekeeping, and be certain to keep accurate records of all transactions starting in 1999.

In addition, prepare your family for your possible long-term unemployment. Spend time talking about the process and discussing the changes you expect to take place. Remember, Noah spent 100 years preparing for an event no one else believed could ever happen. Perhaps no other single event is as predicable as Y2K, so do your part now in order to ensure your needs will be met and your family will be cared for.

Your Y2K Planning Guide

Ten Steps to Prepare Yourself for a Career Change

1. Have yourself tested to reveal your talents and skills.
2. Purchase a book on career choices and read it.
3. Sit down with friends and ask them for honest feedback as to your job possibilities.
4. Make a detailed list of your past employment positions.
5. List your educational history. Be sure to include formal classes, degrees, night classes, special-interest seminars, and hobbies.
6. Don't overlook your life experiences. The very experiences that give us confidence to face hard times can also help us discover new areas for possible employment.
7. Get letters of recommendation updated. Remember that hard times can bring out the best or the worst in people. Employers will be looking for honest, trustworthy, and dependable people.
8. Interview friends who have careers you find interesting.
9. Call a technical school and go visit. Practical skills will be important if we suffer a depression.
10. Draw up an excellent in-depth resumé.

SIXTEEN

Education and Activities

Does Y2K mean no school? For years school districts from elementary to secondary to community colleges and on through to universities have eagerly pushed ahead with the computerization of every facet of their institutions. Most of the things administrators used to do on paper are now computer-generated. An interruption of electricity will shut down those computers, obviously, but a more insidious problem will be the date-sensitive information and records. All Y2K problems that affect the software and records will hurt the institution and its ability to operate effectively.

If electric power and other utilities are disrupted, *most schools have no alternative but to shut down.* It's questionable whether schools can continue operating without telephone service for more than a few days. If food supplies for school lunches are disrupted, if the teachers can't travel to the school campus because of breakdowns in the transportation

What's Ahead

• **How Schools Are Affected**

• **Where Will They Go?**

• **A Guide for School Safety**

• **What's a Parent to Do?**

• **The Two- to Three-Day Plan**

• **The One-Month Plan**

• **The One-Year Plan**

• **Your Y2K Planning Guide**

systems, or if school buses are unavailable to bring children to the schools, local elementary schools will be hard-hit.

How Schools Are Affected

The best-case scenario is that schools will not suffer an interruption. Coming at the tail end of the annual Christmas break, a few days of extra vacation due to Y2K will be similar to missing school due to "snow days"—buses can't run, people can't travel, so school is canceled for a day or two. (Children everywhere will rejoice!) However, the worst-case scenario is that power will be out for an extended period, teachers and support staff will be unable to travel, and the education system will shut down. Records could be lost or corrupted due to software glitches, meaning your child's educational history may not be available. Extensive problems would affect your child's educational progress. Can you make it educating your own children?

Large school districts and universities often have computer systems as complex and widespread as a medium-sized business—school lessons, homework assignments, student-teacher communications, research, and scheduling of administrative activities are all driven by computer programs. Not every school is so heavily dependent on computers, of course. Some only have computers in labs, to be used once a week in "computer appreciation" courses. However, *most universities and large high schools are so thoroughly wired that if the computers shut down, the administration might as well turn off the lights.* In a very short time the institution will come close to shutting down.

Other areas of heavy computerized school application include assigning students and teachers to classes and arranging scheduling—an enormously complicated process for high school and college students. Doing the task without the aid of a computer would be a monumental chore, and considerable delays would be likely. Keep in mind that school revenues come from a local school district, which is augmented by monies received from state and local governments. These funds are derived from property taxes at the local level and income taxes at the state and federal levels. Numerous forms of grants and subsidies for school lunches, student loans, scholarships, and research grants to teachers are computer-driven and therefore extremely vulnerable to Y2K problems, particularly if the stream of payments to the government is interrupted for weeks or months. Some institutions may have sufficient reserve funds to complete the current terms, but due to an interruption of funds they would be unable to open in the fall of 2000.

Where Will They Go?

For many adults, school is the day-care provider for their children, the "job" at which the kids work, and if closed due to Y2K problems, parents will be faced with a number of issues: Who will watch the kids while the parents are at work? Who will step in to educate the children until the schools can reopen? And who will take responsibility for reestablishing local schools if parents are too busy rearranging their lives due to Y2K difficulties? Working parents easily remember their children's last extended vacation and the plans they needed to put in place for baby-sitting. Older high school and college students can look after themselves, but one of the serious side effects of a moderate, monthlong Y2K disruption is that *parents will have to cope with the equivalent of a second summer vacation.*

An adult might be willing to tolerate physical discomforts and dangers due to Y2K, but exposing children to the same difficulties is quite another matter. A parent might put up with a lack of heat in the office, or a lack of public transportation for traveling to the office, but won't stand for a six- or seven-year-old child having to live under a similar hardship.

Required curriculum might not be fully covered, therefore the school year might have to be extended. A longer disruption could mean many students have to repeat a year of school. Tuition payments for colleges and private schools are critical funds for these institutions, and if parents cannot pay or want their money back when the institution shuts down, the schools will be significantly hurt. The impact of Y2K computer problems on the field of education may not be as fundamental and serious as the impact on other parts of the economy or social infrastructure, but it is serious enough we can't ignore it. Parents of young children especially need to be concerned.

Most schools survive because of direct funding provided by three levels of government bureaucracy. As with current forms of Social Security, unemployment benefits, food stamps, Medicare, and welfare benefits, current mechanisms for funding schools and subsidizing students could be interrupted for the long term. There are ongoing debates about the ineffectiveness of education spending and initiatives at the federal level, with periodic proposals that the Department of Education be eliminated entirely. Many states have been faced with steadily shrinking budgets, which in turn have forced cutbacks throughout many state universities whose attractiveness is at least partly due to the low tuition costs enjoyed by state residents. Battles over funding at the local level continue, with scattered incidents of budget cutbacks.

American parents will never decide to stop educating their children, regardless of the crisis, and it is doubtful they will be willing to give up the notion of state-sponsored education for all. But with government bureaucracy paralyzed and the House and Senate leaders voted into office in November wanting to focus emergency aid on more pressing issues like providing food and jobs, parents may need to deal with the long-term education needs of their children. Control and funding of the nation's school systems could revert entirely to the local level, at least for the next year or two. Affluent neighborhoods—those able to acquire funding directly from parents and local property owners—might welcome this change. However, urban and rural areas whose school systems are heavily dependent on government funding could find themselves in an extremely difficult situation.

The long awaited reexamination and overhaul of the nation's educational system could come out of a severe Y2K crisis. By the year 2010, a nationwide school system with uniform curriculum and testing standards for both students and teachers, administered by a newly chartered federal agency, could be in place. On the other hand, the exact opposite could also exist: Local agencies could take over the coordination of schools in light of a government shutdown, meaning the federal government would play no role at all in deciding how our children should be educated. This would mean schools have far less funding authority than they have now, but it leaves open the question of whether the educational system would be transformed into something better, or something far worse.

If Y2K does turn out to be severe, it might be a matter of months before the reality becomes widely accepted. Unrelated crises in business or government could eventually trigger the kind of economic upheaval that would lead to severe budget cutbacks and policy changes, even if schools escape any immediate problems. In the face of disruptions, flexibility and self-sufficiency will be extremely important for making it through whatever length of time is necessary. You will want to make it as easy for your family as possible, so having a plan for your children's education is essential. It will give you the edge you will need to pull together with your family and others in your neighborhood to successfully weather the storm.

A Guide for School Safety

Five days a week you put your kids in the care of other people for protection and education. To maintain peace of mind in the case of disruption at school, *keeping them safely at home is the best arrangement.* We suggest you contact your school and get a copy of its emergency plan. Review the plan and ask questions of the person who will be responsible for discipline and order. Know the person's name, telephone number, and extension. If the phones are out, have an agreed-upon plan written and in his hands and with your children. Tape it in their lockers, if you must. Laminate a copy and put it in their backpacks, so your children know what to do in case of an emergency.

Consider how you will contact your children, where you will meet them, and what you will do. Talk with their teachers about emergency teaching plans, and with the principal about plans for food, water, and power. What are the guidelines for discipline and order during an emergency? Can students leave campus without parents picking them up? If they are close to home, can they walk? Do they need to check out? What emergency medical plans are in place? Do teachers know and have they been trained in first aid or CPR? Are emergency medical cards up-to-date on all your students, and are emergency phone numbers and insurance information readily accessible?

Thinking through the provisions for some sort of social upheaval is necessary to do before the emergency takes place. If others at your school are concerned about the effects of Y2K, get together and discuss a contingency plan that involves parents, teachers, and support staff. Make sure to explore provisions for instruction, safety, and snacks or lunches. You may decide to write a letter to the school administrator, outlining briefly any special plans or instructions you deem important. Keep a copy for your records, and talk with your children about the changes Y2K could bring to their schooling.

What's a Parent to Do?

Taking control of your child's learning can be frightening until you realize you already have many of the skills and much of the knowledge needed to help your child succeed. Consider these facts:

- You have a history of parent/teacher conferences.
- You know how to ask good questions, understand problems, and translate the needed improvements into concrete steps at home.
- You have a solid understanding of the classes taught in today's schools—you know the basics of reading, math, history, and science.
- At the elementary level, you are confident you can help your child with homework and projects.

- You have probably observed curriculum changes and your child's ability to adapt to new situations in his or her learning. Moving from grade to grade has brought yearly changes in difficulty of material as well as social skills and friends; your child has adjusted and so have you. In fact, *you are the main reason your kids have successfully made it through those phases.*
- You have helped your children solve problems on projects, special reports, and with low grades or missing assignments. In fact, you probably have a history of success in working with your child's education.

What will be missing if you need to bear the burden of your child's education is probably summed up in three words: confidence, materials, and planning. You may lack the confidence to teach your own children, especially if education isn't your career. However, keep in mind that the skills and talents you have used in your own learning can be drawn upon to help you teach your children. Upper-level studies may scare you a bit, particularly if you weren't a good student in high school. But many students at this level are self-motivated and with encouragement can progress on their own. So even if advanced math scares you, between books, friends, and neighbors, you can generally find someone who has the skills to fill in the gaps of your child's education.

If the public schools are shut down and textbooks are not available, materials can still be found at libraries and homeschool stores. More than one million homes already have chosen to homeschool their children in this country, and chances are you already know someone who homeschools and can put you in touch with the educational resources you need. Ask some people if you can look through their materials. How do they teach their children? What curriculum are they using, where did they get it, and how much did it cost? What are their biggest problems? If they were to start over, what would they do differently? The answers to these questions should help you see that if you needed to, you could become your child's teacher.

Planning your child's education might be your toughest task. Get out an old report card and you will find the subjects you'll need to cover. If you need to get your child through an entire semester, or even a complete year, map out a course of study. This isn't difficult—simply take the number of pages in the textbook and divide it by the number of days you will have to complete the work. Your child will have to complete those number of pages daily in order to finish the course on time. Plan in your number of days, tests, and review times, making everything bite-sized. Networking with other parents will reap skills you may lack, so be willing to work with other parents who have children the same ages as your own.

Knowing you can succeed is important. By putting a plan into place, having materials on hand, and talking to people who have already worked at homeschooling, you'll quickly get a feel for what it's like to educate your children in your home. Help your kids to grow by encouraging reading and having good books on your bookshelves, learn to use your encyclopedia for things you don't know, and keep a positive attitude. Not only can you take charge of your child's learning, you'll even find it fun and exciting.

The Two- to Three-Day Plan

Several days of not being able to go to school will not be a great hardship—for elementary and secondary students it will be an extended Christmas break. Your family will no doubt survive without too much trouble. The difficulty depends on the breakdown of utilities and other goods and services you might rely on when your children have extra free time. Activities like going to the mall, watching movies, or playing video games will need to be adjusted if the electricity is out. Travel of any sort could be troublesome. You may be spending extra time getting your own household to maintain order and finding interesting ways to while away the time.

College students are likely to be enjoying an extended break, but may be employed over Christmas and not know what will occur at their institution if Y2K creates serious problems. Ask the college for its plan before leaving school in December, and be wary of paying significant up-front costs before January 1, 2000.

The One-Month Plan

If Y2K turns out to be severe, you may have to deal with a month of no school at all. If that is the case, have a contingent baby-sitting plan in place, especially if both parents work. Older siblings, grandparents, neighbors, or other parents may be available to help you put a child-care plan in place. The key is to have a network of sympathetic and like-minded parents or family members before January 1, 2000, rather than waiting to see if you can create something after the fact. Don't depend on government-sponsored day-care centers, since they're likely to have problems of their own.

A one-month disruption may affect the number of days your school requires and the amount of material needed to be covered in order to complete the school year. If extended problems force schools to close for a period of time, extending the school year into the summer months may be a real possibility. Some school districts could expect students to catch up on homework, reading assignments, and written reports on their own time. Plan to meet with your child's teachers late in 1999 and get a project assignment plan in writing to insure your child will be on target and well-prepared when school resumes.

Remember that you'll be coping with your own disruptions as well as your child's educational choices, so allow extra time to cope with the demands of the Y2K problem. Keep a daily record of schoolwork completed, provide a place for all assignments to be kept neat and easily accessible when school resumes, and take time to work with your kids so that schoolwork doesn't become a drudgery. Spending time together playing games and doing fun activities is just as important as completing every history assignment.

The One-Year Plan

It seems unbelievable that schools in America could be closed for a year, but if a school district's budget is exhausted, the education of your children will be left entirely up to you. Have a plan for what you'll be doing.

First, get over the shock. Many schools now operate on thin budgets, and any breakdown in the money flow could easily cause severe problems. School discipline, frail as it is, could unravel and force a shutdown. There may be very little in the way of a "reserve buffer" to deal with extraordinary problems. If the payroll computers break down, the teachers, custodians, and administrators won't get paid, so it won't take long for the affected workers to go on strike or look for other jobs. If several months go by, the school district may find it easiest to simply terminate the school year in order to regroup for the next year.

Long-term child-care will be needed, as will some sort of alternative schooling option. Find out if your public school textbooks could be used for your students at home, and if they could receive credit for completed work. If you must be the teacher and supply your own texts, have some basic reading, science, history, and math books in your home. Home schooling is a growing, popular option with many Christian families—perhaps it is right for you. Use the table of contents to offer guidelines for doing research and writing. Have your children write journals, essays, poetry, and short stories as part of their learning. If you think you're going to be in charge of your child's education, consider getting in touch with the National Home School Association and the National Home School Legal Defense Fund.

YOUR Y2K PLANNING GUIDE

15 Things Your Child Should Study at Home

1. Reading (keep good books on hand)
2. Grammar (look for an introductory guide)
3. Handwriting (practice on lined paper)
4. Spelling (use a guide or simply select words from novels)
5. Vocabulary (have them keep track of new words in novels)
6. Writing (simply ask them to write stories and reports)
7. Math (use an age-appropriate textbook)
8. Science and nature studies (look for a book that relies on your house and neighborhood, rather than on expensive props)
9. Geography (an atlas and some maps will do)
10. History (reading good history books is essential)
11. Government (explore the Constitution with your kids)
12. Economics (help them earn and save money)
13. Bible (read and discuss Bible stories with them)
14. Art (colored pencils, watercolors, and paper are all you need)
15. Music (help them gain an appreciation for singing or playing instruments)

SEVENTEEN

Making a Home

It's our job to create happy memories with our kids, even if we are experiencing serious societal troubles. They need to grow up with the opportunity to have fun, enjoy each other, and laugh with their mom and dad. As mothers and fathers, we've been given the wonderful opportunity to create joyful memories in the lives of our children. When we take the time to do something special with them, or relive a moment, or enjoy a family tradition, it builds and affirms the unity of our families. Studies have shown that children who know they belong and are appreciated in their families do better in school, have a stronger self-image, and are far more likely to have a healthy, successful marriage. Even in times of societal breakdown, our families can be strong.

God designed the family as the foundation for society. He intended parents to be the craftsmen who mold the children into adulthood, helping them adjust and succeed in life. That's the greatest responsibility a parent has—*to know we are called to shape our children*. And the greatest joy we have is to watch our kids walk

What's Ahead

- **Family Night**
- **Fostering Personal Growth**
- **The Fun Kit**
- **Conversation Starters**
- **The Two- to Three-Day Plan**
- **The One-Month Plan**
- **The One-Year Plan**
- **Your Y2K Planning Guide**

212 • The Y2K Family Survival Guide

in the truth. When parents invest time and energy into their children, they are making an eternal investment. The leaders who have positively influenced the world most have come from strong, healthy homes. In the face of a Y2K crisis, the need for strong family bonds will be even more powerful. We don't claim to have perfect children, nor to have worked out every detail, but we have discovered that it is possible to help shape our kids through strong relationships and activities. Even with teenagers, it is possible to maintain a healthy friendship and offer welcome input into their lives. And the secret of success is simple: Learn to invest time and have fun. If you're willing to do a few simple things, you can succeed.

First, spend time *talking* with your son or daughter—it may be an effort at first, especially for dads, but the rewards are worth the investment. Talk about "favorites"—favorite days, favorite activities, favorite people—and find out what your children are thinking. Discuss people and events with them so they gain your mature perspective on the world. Tell about your life, your feelings, and your ideas so that your children feel they know and understand you. By your doing so, they will learn to open up and discuss their own feelings and dreams. A family that talks together keeps the lines of communication open, even when there are disagreements and disappointments.

Second, spend time building *traditions*. Give your children a sense of expectation for what will happen on birthdays and holidays. Help them appreciate their heritage. A sense of personal identity may be built on the choices a young person makes, but those choices rest on the traditions the parents have laid as a foundation.

Third, spend *time* doing nothing. Having fun at ball games, baking, and reading books can be just as important as filling up the schedule with activities. They won't remember the deal you closed or the money you made, but they'll always remember the time you spent with them. If you focus on those three words—*talking, tradition,* and *time*—you're halfway home.

Family Night

It doesn't take a genius to make a memory. It just takes a parent willing to spend a few minutes thinking up a good idea. For example, if you are together as a family with time on your hands due to Y2K, think of an activity or game you can do. Create a family tree, build a birdhouse or bookshelves, make a quilt, start a garden, have a family talent show, cook your meals together, or tell family stories. It's going to take faith to survive Y2K, so go to church together. Read your Bible to your kids and pray for them. There is no end to the special memory-making activities you can invent, if you put your mind to it. *Decide that you're going to create happy memories in the lives of your children, even during a time of national crisis, and you'll soon find your days are filled with meaningful activities.* Whether you're a single mom or the father of a tribe, you can create family memories that will be enjoyed anywhere—in a home, apartment, duplex, mobile home, or huge estate. The size of your family, like the size of your income, doesn't matter . . . only the size of your heart.

For many parents, the most important lesson they can learn is *how to have a good time.* Perhaps with all the expectations and responsibilities of parenthood, you've forgotten what it's like to have fun. To those people, we suggest pondering what made fun and games so enjoyable as kids—running around, chasing each other, touching, laughing, and throwing things. In one sense, those are the essential elements of any good game. When the family can spend time together and have fun, it makes for a more happy family and better-adjusted kids.

You'll discover games can also be useful for building skills in the lives of your children. Learning about sports and strategy, as well as character qualities like judgment and honesty, is best done within the context of family games. Not only that, games offer you time together when family members can learn about each other. Sometimes in a game your kids will be called upon to help someone else, to cheer others on, or to build them up, and that fosters family unity.

We regularly enjoy sitting down to board games at the kitchen table and having everyone participate. When our children were small, their favorites were Candy Land, Memory, Mousetrap, Hot Potato, and Operation. As they got older, they enjoyed Yahtzee, Uno, Racko, Trouble, Clue, Sorry, Battleship, Monopoly, Life, and Aggravation. Some people like word games—like Scrabble, Password, Boggle, and Upwards—while others prefer strategy games like Risk and Mastermind. Some great new games have come out in recent years that are a lot of fun: Guesstures, Taboo, Pictionary, Balderdash, and Scattergories are all winners. You'll also find that some versions of Trivial Pursuit and the various other trivia games can be both fun and educational.

Think about the classic games you played as a child: hide and seek, kick the can, freeze tag, frisbee golf, steal the bacon, capture the flag, and king of the hill. Get a basketball and play "horse," play catch with a baseball, or set up an obstacle course. Build a slip-and-slide, make gifts for people, or build and fly a kite. Nearly every child enjoys charades, Ping-Pong, pillow fights, paper airplane shows, follow the leader, Twister, balloon games, and simply wrestling on the floor with Daddy. Not all games have to wreck the furniture, of course. Your kids can quietly draw pictures; play tic-tac-toe, Simon Says, or 20 Questions; or put together jigsaw puzzles. You can establish some wonderful memories just by having fun and playing games with your kids.

Fostering Personal Growth

You have a remarkable opportunity to pass on skills to your children. Kids need to learn all sorts of things, from reading to personal hygiene, and you have been put in charge of the lessons. Your home is the best school your child will ever attend. When you purposefully choose to foster talent in your kids, you not only build unity in your home, but also help shape their lives and prepare them for the future. Skill-building is a blessing since it allows you time with your child, focused on his or her future success.

Helping children learn things also allows you to create a unique expression of your family. If your strengths are in music and speaking, you can help your kids learn how to get up and perform in front of a group. If you have skills in crafts and woodworking, you're presented with an opportunity to nurture those same skills in your children. The teaching/learning relationship between you and your child draws both of you closer together, provides the child with a sense of order in the family, and reminds him that home is a safe refuge in a complex world. Think about the things you know that are unique, interesting, or practical, and begin making a plan to share your skill with your kids.

Novels are another wonderful tool for growth. They help us visit other lands, discover other eras, and break a big, complex world into small, understandable parts. Through the printed page we find out about other cultures, learn about various disciplines, and visit new worlds. The best way to foster a love of reading is to read aloud to your children. Sit with them in the evening, open a book, and enjoy with them some of your favorite stories. Use different voices for the various characters, and bring some drama to your reading. Help your kids develop a love for language and writing, an appreciation for good words and ideas, and a creative imagination. If you start reading to them when they're little and read regularly, using a wide variety of books, you'll find your children will continue to enjoy books on their own. It's best to talk about the story afterward, to see what they think and how they respond to the plot and the people. Help them to see that reading is *fun*. Read aloud to your children, and you'll foster silent reading as they grow.

Little children like books by Mercer Mayer, John Goodall, Margery Williams, Jean de Brunhoff, Doctor Suess, Beatrix Potter, H. A. Rey, and Munro Leaf. The poetry of Robert Louis Stevenson and Shel Silverstein is also good, as are the stories of Harry Allard and James Marshall. For older kids, help them explore the novels and stories of A. A. Milne, C. S. Lewis,

Kenneth Grahame, Laura Ingalls Wilder, Robert Louis Stevenson, Ludwig Bemelmans, and Lewis Carroll. Mature readers will enjoy L. Frank Baum, George MacDonald, Lucy Maud Montgomery, Louisa May Alcott, and James Herriott. Reading classic novels is important, so encourage your family to read J. R. R. Tolkien, William Shakespeare, Charles Dickens, Mark Twain, Frances Hodgson Burnett, E. B. White, Beverly Cleary, Howard Pyle, and Anna Sewell.

Something you'll probably find to be true is that if you like one book from an author, you'll like others also. So if you liked *Little Women*, make sure to check out Alcott's *Little Men* and *An Old Fashioned Girl*. If you enjoyed *Treasure Island*, you'll doubtless like *The Black Arrow*. And if you start on the first of the *Chronicles of Narnia*, you will want to read all of them. There are a number of *Dr. Doolittle* and *Madeline* and *Oz* books your kids will enjoy, and as you talk about them with your kids you'll soon discover they become literary critics, able to tell a good story from a weak one. You'll also find that tastes vary, even in children. Listen to what they're telling you and it will help shape your choice of words.

There are a few good treasuries—collections of children's stories that have been put together into one volume. The best one (which we consider a necessity) is *The World Treasury of Children's Literature*, put together by Clifton Fadiman, one of America's best editors. It contains classic stories from all over the globe, together with the original art. The book is published in both hard and soft covers, and you're bound to find a used set at a bookstore. Other good collections include William Bennett's *Book of Virtues*, William Russell's *Classics to Read Aloud*, Andrew Lang's *Blue Fairy Book*, and Isaac Bashevis Singer's *Children's Stories*. You'll also probably want to read *Fairy Tales* by Hans Christian Anderson and the Brothers Grimm, and *Fables* by Aesop. Kenneth Taylor put together 184 illustrated one-paragraph accounts of the major Old and New Testament stories in *The Bible in Pictures for Little Eyes*. It's a nice way to introduce your children to Bible reading. We think reading Scripture regularly is important to our children, and have found they respond best to the language in *Today's English Version* and *The Living Bible*.

If your children enjoy reading a series of books in order to follow a handful of characters, we heartily recommend the writings of Bill Myers, who creates titles like *My Life as a Squashed Burrito*. Many kids like Paul Hutchen's *Sugar Creek Gang*, Paul White's *Jungle Doctor*, Bernard Palmer's *Danny Orliss* series, and Frank Peretti's excellent *Cooper Kids Adventure Series*. If your children are interested in reading a series, you may want to start them with something easy like *The Boxcar Children*. Though not necessarily great literature, these series offer a pleasant mystery and introduce kids to the idea of following characters over time. Many girls enjoy the *Nancy Drew* mysteries, just as boys will like the *Hardy Boys*, *Tom Swift*, and *Encyclopedia Brown* series. Don't allow your kids to read only dime-store series books. Challenge them with great writers and great themes. For young adults, we heartily recommend anything by Jane Austen or the Bronte sisters. They are well-written, uplifting stories of courage and character. Teens will also like *The Diary of Anne Frank*, *The Autobiography of Helen Keller*, and *Sophie's World*—books that offer history and reflection as well as a good story.

Finally, we would like to encourage you to have your kids read history as well as fiction. Though history textbooks have acquired a bad name during the last 30 years, many history books are well-written and offer families a chance to explore events and people in a way fiction doesn't allow. Time-Life has created a wonderful series of educational books on such things as the Old West, space travel, and the Civil War, and your family can spend hours enjoying (and learning) together about our world.

The Fun Kit

In the midst of the mess, you want to be able to feel you are prepared, physically and emotionally, and that you can keep your family together. You want to be able to feel you've still got a "home," even if you decide it's best to relocate someplace temporarily. In earlier chapters our focus was on basic preparation for an emergency—the tools, utensils, and personal things you'll need to survive. What we haven't talked about is the *emotional impact of a crisis and the ways to counter the impact.* Well-being and morale ought to be considered important parts of the survival package, but usually aren't. The military understands the significance of morale. Rest and relaxation are an important element in military operations. The main purpose of organizations like the USO is to keep spirits up and relieve the stress and tension of battle.

What this means is you need to plan for activities that will help ease the anxiety and boredom. The anxiety is caused by the unpredictable nature of the event. During a crisis situation the uppermost question in most people's minds is, "What will happen to us?" The point of planned activities is to distract the mind from constant worry. Boredom is also a factor, since our normal diversions—the CD player, the VCR, and the TV—won't work. Telephones may be out, and we need to save the radio time, so it's important to prepare for the eventuality of having too much time. What will you do with downtime?

Psychologists agree that boredom can be a major problem in an emergency. There are six tactics to diminish boredom. The first is to establish a routine—a pattern of living—and daily activities. The second is to develop a positive attitude. You need to find solutions for the problems that confront you and know that you will survive. The third is to understand the difference between worry and concern. Worry is a negative, but concern is a positive. Worry is a form of fear, while concern is a form of desire to find solutions. The fourth is to take care of yourself and your health. This means we all need to eat and drink regularly and get some form of exercise. The fifth is to keep busy. Idleness promotes gloom. The sixth and final tactic is to be supportive of others. After all, we are in this emergency together, and it's best if we work with each other and help one another.

We suggest you put together, in addition to all your other emergency supplies, a fun kit. The purpose of this kit is to have some things on hand that will provide entertainment and diversion. Use it to offset the advent of falling morale and depression. In an emergency situation, no matter how well we have provided for ourselves, we are living in a most traumatic state.

What you put in your fun kit will be an entirely personal choice. We recommend things that will help you stay positive, healthy, and active. Possible suggestions include books you've always wanted to read but never did, art and craft projects like water colors or knitting or modeling clay, and a diary for keeping a log of your experiences. For young children we suggest favorite toys, puzzles, games, and cards. A jump rope, a football, and things which promote healthy activity and exercise are another good idea. In a time of great stress you will want to have spiritually uplifting reading and study materials available.

Putting your fun kit together should be an enjoyable family project and an opportunity to further discuss the future. Packing the kit can be approached as a challenge: What five fun things would you take with you if you couldn't have anything else? Electronic things and space-consuming items are ruled out. After making your selections, pack away the items so they are ready for use. A good-sized suitcase or small footlocker would be a handy storage container for your fun kit.

Conversation Starters

Conversations with your children are some of the most important parenting activities you can do. The fact that you go into their room, sit on their bed, and talk with them about life is the single greatest opportunity you have. It builds trust, shows your children you think they are important, and keeps the lines of communication open as they experience complex situations. Our culture says that parents and teens can't communicate. We say that's balderdash—parents just give up too easily.

It isn't easy getting a kid to talk, especially if the two of you haven't established a pattern of in-depth conversations. Your children are sure to wonder what your agenda is and why you suddenly seem so interested in their opinions. That's OK. Just start talking with them and see what happens. Of course, right now the males reading this book are wondering, "But what do I say?" Our advice is simple: When in doubt, ask questions. Don't play the role of inquisitor, but use questions to get the ball rolling. For example:

Ask their favorite. What is each child's favorite team, movie, book, song, color, cartoon character, music group, or subject in school? What's the best thing they've ever done or seen or experienced? Talk to them about their dreams and ideas, and be interested in the answers.

Ask their opinion. What are your children's opinions on a subject? What would they like to do when they grow up, or when they go to the fair, or when they have a day off? What do they think about the things going on in the world?

Ask for information. Don't assume you know everything about their lives. Try to get information when you've got something planned, so you know what your children's expectations are. That way your kids get to talk, and you get to see what's on their minds.

Talk at the table. Have something in mind when you all sit down to dinner together. Ask about school, or their day, or be ready to quiz them on a subject. Rose Kennedy used to list a topic on a blackboard each morning, informing her children that whatever was written would be the subject of conversation at the dinner table. It not only kept the lines of communication open, it also got family members thinking about important ideas. One of her children grew up to be president of the United States, another became attorney general, and a third became a U.S. senator—which isn't a bad return on her investment in communication.

Tell your kids about yourself. Share your stories with your children. What happened to you when you were a kid? How was your childhood different than theirs? Although TV shows make fun of Dad droning on about "when I was a child," the truth is that most kids are interested in their parents' lives.

Keep a positive attitude. Don't be too quick to judge your children's answers. They may be trying on an idea to see how it fits. A warm, supportive attitude that exudes interest and caring rather than criticism and constant correction will keep kids talking—and that's what you want most.

The Two- to Three-Day Plan

A short-term emergency will not be as emotionally trying as a longer-lasting one. The initial impact of the crisis and the realization it did in fact occur may come as a slight shock, but if you've made plans, your family should handle it well. The tasks involving food, water, heat, and light should engage everyone and keep them busy.

Meal preparation, for example, could take a lot of time and energy depending on how elaborate your meal plans are. You might need to do such things as start the cooking fire, find the supplies, unpack them, cut and prepare the food, then cook it. After the meal you'll need to clean the utensils, take care of garbage, and put away your supplies. There are a lot of small, time-consuming tasks required in a survival situation, and all this activity will keep you busy and focused. Hopefully by the time you have established some kind of daily routine for dealing with the required chores and are beginning to find time to worry, the emergency will be over.

The One-Month Plan

In a prolonged emergency you will need to figure out ways to keep your spirits up and keep from being bored, especially if you are by yourself or only with one other person. Large families will be better off emotionally because of the amount of work required to support the larger number of people and because of the natural emotional support a family structure offers. Having daily tasks will help keep you busy and organized, but once you have set up a working schedule and things are running smoothly you'll find you have more time than you anticipated. The fun kit will now be appreciated. It should supply you with activities to divert your family.

One project that's appropriate for a month-long emergency is keeping a log or diary. Details of daily experiences, a description of your thoughts and reactions, and an inventory of remaining supplies are possible elements for your diary.

Book-reading is another pastime that will appeal to many people. In our daily lives we often regret we don't have enough time to read, but a month-long emergency can be seen as a wonderful opportunity to catch up on the books we've wanted to break open. Most people have bookshelves in their dwelling, so instead of taking up precious storage space with books in your emergency storage area, make sure you have plenty of books you want to read on your shelves.

We also believe physical activity is an important part of one's health, so use some of your spare time to exercise. It might be as simple as taking a walk or jogging, or you might find you can play some sport like basketball or Frisbee. Children can become bored very quickly, so it is important that you plan activities for them. Keep them occupied and happy, or your situation can deteriorate into a negative, depressing atmosphere. A month-long crisis can be emotionally, physically, and mentally draining even in the best of circumstances, so you want to do everything you can to replenish yourself. Be thankful you prepared for the crisis by having survival supplies and strategies.

The One-Year Plan

After several months, the emergency will cease to be interpreted as a crisis and be accepted as standard living conditions. Daily routines and chores will be well-established. Everyone will know what is required of them and when it needs to be done.

If you relocated to the country from the city before Y2K happened, you already altered your lifestyle. Once the crisis began you were prepared and able to deal with it better than most. For people who decided to leave the city only after Y2K occurred, life will be much harsher and more difficult, and for those still in the cities after a year's time, simply surviving each day may become a challenge. We need to remind you that family flexibility, mobility, and liquidity are the key elements to existence under these conditions.

YOUR Y2K PLANNING GUIDE

*20 Questions to Strike Up Conversations with your Kids:**

1. What is your favorite food?
2. Tell me about the neatest birthday present you ever received.
3. What makes you laugh?
4. Where would you like to go for a vacation if you could go any-place in the whole world?
5. If you had to move and could take only three things with you, what would you take?
6. Describe the "ideal" father.
7. What is something you can do pretty well?
8. What is your favorite song?
9. What is your best friend like?
10. How would you describe yourself to someone who does not know you?
11. Tell about a time when you felt proud of yourself.
12. What kind of store would you like to own and operate?
13. If you received 5000 dollars as a gift, how would you spend it?
14. What is your favorite room in your house? Why?
15. What kind of a job do you want to have in 20 years?
16. What talent do you wish you had?
17. If someone could give you anything in the world for your birthday, what would you like it to be?
18. What would you like to invent to make life better?
19. What is something that "bugs" you?
20. What kind of trophy would you like to win?

---

* These questions and some of the information in this chapter are taken from *Family Times* by Jerry and Patti MacGregor (Harvest House Publishers, 1998). You can find a copy at your favorite bookstore.

EIGHTEEN

Love Thy Neighbor

I n any crisis, your family and neighbors become the most important people in your life. However, waiting until the emergency happens isn't a good idea. Take steps now, even small ones, to help you, your family, and your neighbors maintain order in times of disorder.

All of us have at one time or another had to deal with an emergency—a death in the family, an accident at school, or car problems on the freeway. Thinking through these emergencies will help prepare us for Y2K. We suggest you review a past emergency to help you get a picture of what could happen if a disastrous situation arises:

- How did you and your family handle the problem? Was there panic? Did everyone know how to reach each other? Was there any problem contacting one another?

- Was there a plan on what to do or where to meet? Did you have a list of emergency telephone numbers, and numbers of relatives, friends, and neighbors?

- How disruptive was the emergency? Did you or

What's Ahead

- **Won't You Be My Neighbor?**

- **Are You a Leader?**

- **Your Neighbors, Your Friends**

- **The Two- to Three-Day Plan**

- **The One-Month Plan**

- **The One-Year Plan**

- **Your Y2K Planning Guide**

someone else have to travel away from home? Was there ample money for the emergency?

- Did you know how to handle the problems that arose? Problems like air travel, motels, car rental, and long-distance phone calls in times of trouble can be major obstacles to restoring peace and order.
- How long did it take you and your family to "get back to normal"?

Looking at past crises will not solve any future emergencies, but will help you plan for the future. As you reflect on the past event and how it affected you, your family, and your budget, it can help you decide how you want to prepare for any future emergencies.

The fact is, nobody plans for emergencies—they just happen. But Y2K is unique. We know it's coming, we can identify some of the repercussions of it, but we won't know exactly what will occur until it is upon us. It's usually in an emergency that we realize our dependency on family, friends, church, neighbors, and our city. When the emergency happens to just you, the love and support from others helps get you through it. But when Y2K hits, we'll all need to depend on one another to survive. The friendships and trust we have with those closest to us will make all the difference in the world.

Won't You Be My Neighbor?

It's easy to say that most modern families live selfish and busy lives. Relationships with neighbors are shallow at best, unfriendly at worst, but most often simply nonexistent. In a time of crisis, strangers are not your best friends. Your neighbors and the relationships you have developed can be the difference between life and death, or hard and easy living. Before the crisis, strengthen your relationships with your neighbors.

Take an active role in organizing your neighborhood. Undesirable groups will form if the law-abiding majority is not forming its own protective groups. Gangs and organized crime can flourish where there is a vacuum of organized leadership. For example, after the fall of the Soviet Union, the Russian mafia seized a chokehold on neighborhoods. The vacuum of local leadership, and the rise of corrupt leadership, were contributing factors to the breakdown of Russian society. A strong neighborhood can resist that.

The groups that are most likely to lead the community out of chaos are neighborhoods and churches. The basic traditional structure of a church keeps leadership from becoming petty tyranny and encourages all members to be servants, doing good works in the spirit of teamwork. The dynamics of church structure are often enough to permit newcomers to bring ideas and energy that add to the existing mission of serving the community. Not all local churches are productive in serving their community, of course. Some are examples of bureaucracy, and you may have had an unfortunate experience with a church that has kept you away for years. However, if you consider yourself an agnostic, have been hurt in a church, or consider yourself too worldly to be welcome in any church, we encourage you to check out a local church. You may be surprised at what you find—especially in a smaller congregation.

Some churches already have plans and are active in caring for weaker members of their community. Plans that help refugees, unemployed members, and the homeless are in place in many churches. In fact, the church in modern history has been a powerful social fixture. Through times of crisis, even a weak church can be made strong. After the defeat of Nazi Germany, when the government and its services were gone and every bureaucrat had been deposed, the church was still there, ministering to those in need. As refugees from East Germany poured into the west, and as the nation tried to rebuild, the churches were the active instruments of health, welfare, education, charity, and local leadership. Pastors who had supported Hitler were gone, but faith in God and service for His kingdom remained.

If U.S. municipal and federal agencies vanish, it will be the churches that remain standing. Communities will begin to look to churches for guidance, help, and direction. Therefore, we urge people to begin praying about the problem, asking for guidance, direction, and wisdom. Strengthen your faith by reading God's Word, searching out verses and passages that give testimony of God's faithfulness in times of trouble. Meet with your pastor and talk to him about your concerns. Consider becoming involved by helping him with gathering information, making plans for meeting the needs of church members, and establishing a system for helping your community.

Are You a Leader?

Y2K can be a wonderful opportunity for leaders to act decisively. It will be an opportunity to prevent anarchy, promote civilized conduct, and rise to the full calling of leadership. If you have a position of authority, you have a calling to lead your congregation and your community. It is a wonderful opportunity to minister, serve, inspire, make disciples, and rebuild. Preparation will prevent panic and fear as some members of society compete for scarce resources. The church will either be discredited or it will prosper, taking leadership in a crisis. If your congregation is not ready to face the potential hardships and turn the situation to the Lord's advantage, it will be a scary time with real dangers. But if people are prepared, the Y2K problem is not to be feared.

As a leader, prepare your people. Encourage them to be ready to assume the responsibilities of civic duty on short notice. Have a group meet and begin to examine the issue of "tough times." Explore what Y2K could do to families and communities, and discuss what practical steps you can take to help those in need. Even if the crisis is short-lived, the church has a great opportunity to minister and assist people who are searching for the truth. The church can distribute unwanted clothing or canned goods to small local charities, get involved in community affairs, offer encouragement to law enforcement, and assist families overcome by the disaster.

One of the jobs of the church is to strengthen the character of the people, so make it a point to inform them about potential hardships and prepare them for an effort to extend hospitality to others. The United States is the most computer-dependent nation on earth, and its people are perhaps the most unprepared for hardship. No one knows what will happen to the civil order if the crisis is severe and recovery takes years. If the character of the American people is weak, undisciplined, and depraved, a panic-stricken populace could beg the government to assume dictatorial powers. But if the church and community leaders are willing to stand in the gap before a general panic, they can rise to a position of service and ministry that will bring peace to the nation and glory to God.

It will take clarity of vision to see the scope and nature of the problem, and patience to explain it in the face of ridicule—the same problems Noah faced for 100 years. People need to be persuaded that the problems are genuine, and it will take leaders of uncommon wisdom to persuade them. A strong, persistent man or woman can help the country remain resolute in the midst of tough decisions, especially those about food and energy distribution. The decisions will be real, and they will be difficult. It will require maturity, prayer, wisdom, and a great deal of cooperation among people to help save a community in disorder. If you're a leader, your country will need you.

Your Neighbors, Your Friends

Home is where you and your family hope to live in peace, safety, and harmony with each other and your neighbors. But do you remember how you reacted to your most recent emergency? Imagine your entire city responding that way to a state of emergency. Under extreme stress, the will to survive knows no bounds. Self-preservation is the strongest urge we humans possess. People under stress can behave like strange, unknown animals. And unfortunately, most people will be totally unprepared. If disaster were to strike, few factories or federal offices will have a plan to aid injured workers or provide for their well-being over a long period of time.

As a concerned person, one who is responsible and interested in the welfare of others, you walk a lonely path. Ask your friends about their emergency Y2K plans and you may be surprised to find you are alone in your preparation. Taking a realistic look at your neighborhood will reap wonderful benefits in your preparedness.

Remember: There is safety in numbers. In a citywide emergency, you don't want to be alone—safety lies in strong relationships with your neighbors. If you live close to retirees, they may need extra help when the power goes down. Create a neighborhood watch group, and let them know you'll be checking on their welfare when the time comes. Organize medical and safety patrols for your neighborhood, and be willing to share information about tools and skills that are important in a crisis. For example, chain saws will be in demand after January 1, but few homes have a working chain saw.

Your neighbors need to become your friends. Monthly meetings could be arranged as a means of getting acquainted and beginning to share ideas. Some people have even begun neighborhood newsletters to help keep everyone up-to-date. There is no one right way or plan, but the fact that you have a plan and have taken action is important.

The Two- to Three-Day Plan

Even if the troubles from Y2K are short-lived, your neighborhood will be important. Gather your family together and ensure their safety and well-being, then check on your neighbors. Contact one other family in your area to see if they are in the same situation as your family. If you have elderly or handicapped neighbors, make a special point of checking with them to make sure they are all right.

Listen to emergency reports in your area, and share that information with friends. If you can all keep warm and well-fed, you'll get through the difficulty.

The One-Month Plan

If you think Y2K will last a month, meet regularly with your neighbors in order to coordinate your neighborhood watch, establish safety patrols, and care for the elderly, handicapped, and shut-ins. We do not recommend sharing the information that you have a supply of food and water, unless you plan to share your supplies with the neighborhood.

Again, if you are making a one-month plan, by all means invest in friendships where you live. Neighborhoods that band together and care for one another will be safer and more secure in the midst of the crisis.

The One-Year Plan

Most people who fear Y2K will last a year or longer have decided to do one of two things: move away or become part of a group. By moving away, they are choosing to become self-reliant. By joining a group, they are choosing to identify themselves with others. If you decide to join with your neighbors, consider buying food supplies in bulk to save costs. You may also want to invest in some sort of water tank for your area, which can hold a large quantity of fresh drinking water. Establish a community garden to provide fresh fruits and vegetables, and make sure it is secure. And by all means, discuss the issues of sharing and protection. With whom will you share your precious resources? How are you willing to protect one another? Advanced decisions on sharing and protection will move your group toward the goal of becoming prepared for Y2K.

YOUR Y2K PLANNING GUIDE

Ten Questions to Consider for Your Neighborhood

1. Do you know your neighbors by name?
2. Do you have their addresses and telephone numbers?
3. When was the last time you talked with them?
4. Do they know you and your family?
5. Do they have your telephone number and other important information?
6. Do you trust them? Do they trust you?
7. Could you confide in them about your needs?
8. Would they come to your assistance?
9. Do they share the same concerns for safety and welfare?
10. Do they have firearms?

NINETEEN

Apartment Life

We recognize that not all families live in single-dwelling homes. Many live in apartments, mobile homes, and condominiums. When confronted with an emergency, those who live in apartments will have particular needs. The fact that a higher concentration of people per square foot live in your housing complex makes survival during and after a disaster more difficult. The construction materials used to build your home were different and lighter, thereby making these structures more easily damaged. Single women who live in flimsy apartments simply won't feel as safe as those who live in a house. Storing supplies and extra survival needs can be extra hard in an apartment. The limited open space can make it harder to band together and bring anyone in to join you.

High-density living situations pose unique problems. Because of the greater number of people in a smaller radius, problems multiply. If there is civil unrest, evacuation from damaged buildings may be more difficult. High-rise apartments increase in danger the higher up you live, and

What's Ahead

- **Creating a Survival Plan**

- **Taking the Lead**

- **What Can You Do?**

- **Getting Around**

- **Colleges and Residential Facilities**

- **The Two- to Three-Day Plan**

- **The One-Month Plan**

- **The One-Year Plan**

- **Your Y2K Planning Guide**

first aid or rescues during a time of disaster are difficult. Authorities may have to find your apartment in a maze of look-alike buildings, the addresses are often hard to find, and an excessive number of cars in a limited area makes it more difficult to get to you. Fire hazards are higher due to the closeness of other buildings. And the responsibility for turning off gas, water, and electric services is vague.

Whether you own a home or live in an apartment, your world will change on January 1, 2000. In these high-concentration population complexes, solutions in times of disaster require a group effort. What will you do? If you are living in one of these housing units, you need a plan designed specifically for apartment-living.

Creating a Survival Plan

Every complex, even in normal times, should have a plan for emergencies. For people who live in apartments, we suggest you begin by compiling a list of your neighbors. Write down their names, addresses, and telephone numbers, being careful to list all family members. Then make a list of their cars, trucks, and vans, noting make and model as well as license plate numbers.

Next, *make an effort to organize your neighbors*. Rather than face panic at the last minute, talk with your neighbors about the potential trouble of Y2K, and explain that you believe people in the complex should stick together. What would happen if no one had any power or water for two weeks? The fact that you live close to each other, sharing the same building, should propel you to decide what to do as a group, rather than as individuals. If there are elderly tenants living in your building, make sure you get their next of kin's names, addresses, and telephone numbers in case of a medical problem or if someone needs to be notified about your neighbor's condition.

Above all, start developing relationships with those closest to you. Be friendly enough with your neighbors to know if they are away out of town, and when they will be back. If you feel particularly close, talk to them about having access to each other's apartments in case of an emergency.

You will also want to survey your immediate physical surroundings. What is the shape, size, layout, and design of your building? Where would you retreat to in an emergency? Is there a "safe" place to go? We recommend having a basic emergency plan you could rely on in case of water-main breaks, power outages, or road closures. Think about where the utility shutoffs are, and who will turn off the gas and electrical power, if need be. That way you'll already be thinking about how you can work together and rely on one another. Think in terms of escape and survival. How could you all get out and survive if there were a fire? Draw a map that shows fire exits, stairways, and hydrants. What is the parking arrangements for tenants, and how are the spaces assigned? If parking spaces are mostly occupied, would they hinder police, fire, or rescue vehicles? Would there be an alternate route into your building?

Your choice of apartments is also important. If you are above the second floor, do you have escape ladders? How many stairways are in your building, and how close are you to the nearest one? Which neighbors live farthest from an escape, and are they elderly, handicapped, or limited in any way? Do any of them work nights and sleep in the daytime? Which units have alarms? You may think this sounds like normal fire or earthquake preparedness, and this plan certainly would be helpful in the face of that type of emergency, but actually what you are doing is bonding together a team of people who trust and rely on one another. That way if Y2K leads to serious societal trouble, the people in your building will be able to watch out and protect each other.

If you are living in a high concentration of housing, apartments, or mobile homes, consider mobilizing teams and working together. Your "people resources" are ample; the problem will be organizing and delegating. A well-thought-out plan with teams assigned and leaders appointed could make the difference between immediate survival or extended hardship. In some cases it could be the difference between life or death. Ask people to serve as leaders, heading up specific areas of need. One person can be in charge of safety, another can handle bulk food-buying, and a third can be the person who keeps in touch with the police and fire departments. Safety patrols in an apartment complex can offer a great deal of security and peace of mind.

One team could locate and check on everyone to see if they are OK and if they have any immediate needs. In the event of disruptions, health problems could be augmented. The elderly need to know they are not alone. If there is actually a serious problem—utilities off, traffic lights out—one team could try and deal with the problem and direct people and traffic while another arranges for shelter and transportation if anyone needs to move. Keep in mind that in any of these situations you could be the one needing the help. Make your plans, prepare, and be willing to help others, but remember that all the effort may be directed to you and meeting your needs. All of the teams could have identifying markings, vests, and flashlights, so people will recognize and respond to them.

There are benefits to apartment living, of course. For one thing, you have neighbors, so you know you won't be alone. The fact that many of you are together can create the safety of numbers, and offers a natural group for bulk food-buying. You can pool your resources to buy and store firewood, and share one apartment if you need to keep together in order to generate heat. If there is a swimming pool, you'll have plenty of potable water. And there is often shared storage, so that several of you can work together to gather the things you'll need to face Y2K.

Taking the Lead

All of this preparation takes money, time, leadership, and cooperation. Unfortunately, most of us are used to being independent and doing everything for ourselves. In apartment complexes, it's easy to hide from neighbors simply because we sense they are too close. It takes time to break down that resistance we have taken so long to build up. Gentle ways, kind words, and encouragement can be keys to drawing others in to help. Don't be discouraged.

Call a meeting of key people—your nearest neighbors, friends, and people you already know. Tell them up front what you want to do, and invite them to be a part of your plan. At the first meeting, brainstorm the needs that would exist in a Y2K crisis. Based on this session, ask people to explore your complex and report back at the next meeting. Somewhere in the process someone will need to *write down the plan*. Ask someone to volunteer, and make sure everyone involved gets a copy.

At a subsequent meeting, deal with the major areas of concern: the immediate need to contact everyone and see if they are OK, to check those requiring medical assistance, and to share information. Remind everyone that it's hard to plan for emergencies. To begin with, we don't like to think about the possibilities. It is uncomfortable thinking about all the hardship we would have to suffer, so it's easier to ignore the situation. But Y2K cannot be ignored, especially if you live alone or have special needs.

Your location in your building is very important to you and your loved ones. Can you get out easily and quickly? If you are higher then the first floor, how would you get out if you needed to? How long would it take? Getting out in an emergency is first priority. Will you need any tools in your apartment or mobile home to help you? Y2K doesn't imply an earthquake or fire, but situations could arise where you would be in danger and needing to leave your residence. To do so, you need a plan. Talk to your neighbors about the tools or equipment you might need, like a camp stove or large ice chest, and decide to go in together on them.

If you have access to a car, assess your parking situation. Is your car safe? Where do you park at night—underground, under a carport, or out in the open? Transportation is a major need during and after an emergency, so talk with your neighbors about how you can watch out and protect each other's vehicles.

If your present parking situation is not ideal, consider an alternative. Is it possible to rent space at a nearby neighbor's home, or is there space available at a secure lot nearby? Some people even look for restaurants, malls, or business parking lots for nighttime parking, knowing they are safer than a dark apartment parking lot.

Additionally, you ought to have some sort of alternative living space if at all possible. Call friends in the country or a family with a wood stove and talk with them about the possibility of joining them at the start of the new year. If you've purchased and packed your food wisely, you should be able to stack it in your vehicle on short notice. You should also consider having some basic emergency supplies with you in your car. That way if you have to leave your city quickly, you'll have a few necessities with you. It isn't difficult to regularly carry with you a small backpack with some survival items in it. Warm clothes, some freeze-dried meals, a flashlight, and a water bottle don't take up much space, but they'll offer you incredible peace of mind as we head toward the new millennium.

What Can You Do?

Why all the fuss? Remember, the ultimate goal is survival for you and your loved ones. No one wants to be standing outside on a cold January morning, unable to stay in their apartment because there is no water, no electricity, and no transportation. Even if Y2K causes only a few days of disruption, your thinking and planning now can save you from starving, freezing, or becoming a victim of criminals. It will require you to be courageous and determined.

Think of it this way: *Under what conditions would your current living place be uninhabitable due to Y2K?* How much damage, how much disruption of utilities would it take to force you out of your home, be it condo, apartment, or mobile home? Some might think there is nothing that could cause them to leave their belongings, the things they have purchased through sweat and tears, but it is possible your building could be completely shut down. Consider an apartment complex ten stories high with no water or electricity—you would have that long climb every time you wanted to go outside. If you are an elderly person living in a mobile home and all your utilities are off, what would you do for heat and light? Could you afford to stay? If you have a baby in your apartment and no heat or running water, do you think you could stay?

Many Y2K experts have examined the giant power blackout that occurred in New Zealand three years ago. Within days, large apartment buildings were vacant. The stench of human waste drove some out, the darkness of inner apartments caused others to leave, and the almost complete lack of security led the few remaining families to seek shelter elsewhere. Criminals worked the streets, looting and breaking into buildings. In that particular case, the power was off almost three weeks. Fortunately, it happened in a warm-weather city, so those sleeping outside were not in danger of dying from exposure. But the incident caused survival experts to conclude that large apartments would not be deemed desirable in a long-term emergency setting.

In a similar circumstance, you probably could find a place to stay for a short time. But what if the problem were extended over a large city, and you were being joined by thousands of others who were also trying to find alternative living sites? How would you survive for several weeks? A tent may be the answer, though it lacks security. You would also need to think about heading to a warm climate and stocking up with various supplies: candles, matches, kerosene lamps or heaters, bottled water, a flashlight, batteries, a battery-operated radio, gloves, shovel, hammer, crowbar, a first-aid kit, large plastic sheets, rope, and trash bags would all be handy.

Basic food for several days might include soup packets, bread, candy, and prepackaged items that do not require heating like nuts, raisins, and dry cereal. If heating water is possible, packaged hot cereals, vegetables, and canned soups and stews would be helpful. Dried foods are great, since they come prepackaged and store for long periods of time, but they can be expensive. A supply of forks, spoons, plates, cups, a knife, a can opener, cooking pans, and charcoal and matches would also be essential. Don't forget to have warm clothing, gloves, extra socks, and a hat. Plastic trash bags could be used if you were out in the rain or wanted to keep out the cold.

Again, a supply of water is critical. Even if you have quantities in your apartment, if you can't get in, they will do you no good. Bottled water is sold in stores, so plan to buy several bottles and have them in your emergency kit. A large plastic container could store all of this in the trunk of your car.

Getting Around

Most cities have some means of public transportation. Buses, trains, and trolleys will take you anywhere you need to go. More and more people are encouraged to use them, but in a Y2K emergency, you can't be sure they will be running. By all means write down your regular routes, look for alternate ways, and be prepared for changes. Regular travelers on public transportation share a common code of ethics. Who to talk to, when to give up your seat, and how to deal with a disruption are more or less understood by seasoned travelers. Twice per day they are in the same bus, going over the same route, bearing the same problem—"How can I get where I want to in the shortest amount of time and with the least hassle?"

As you travel, be keenly aware of what alternatives you would have if public transportation wasn't working. Do you know the route thoroughly? What would be the shortest way home from any point along the way? Could you walk? How long would it take? Would you be safe in the neighborhoods? Do you have money on you? Would you be warm and dry enough? If the answer to any of these questions is no, you need to create a new plan. Make friends with another person who could and would help you.

Planning is preparation, and being prepared gives you the confidence you will need to make it safely to your destination. Carry a small backpack with you, containing an extra pair of socks, a hand towel, a large trash bag, and a small battery-operated radio. You might also want to have a toothbrush and toilet paper with you, and an extra bottle of any medication you are on. A working flashlight and a knife may come in handy, and of course be sure to list your personal information—your name, address, telephone numbers, and next of kin. Above all, be calm and stay positive.

You may want to carry a small supply of food items like gum, granola bars, or trail mix with you at all times. The challenge is no doubt getting all these items into one small space and getting in the habit of carrying them with you, but it's worth the bother. Being prepared when traveling during a crisis can save you time and trouble.

Colleges and Residential Facilities

If you have ever lived in a college dorm, the thought of a disaster is frightening—it's just too large of a group to care for. Hundreds of people share common utilities of water, electricity, heating, and sewage. Most of these students will be away on holiday when Y2K strikes, but many campuses will remain open, and the potential for students being stuck on campus is very real.

The uniqueness of these facilities is that all the people living there are totally dependent on their particular administrators, bosses, or dorm leaders for their complete welfare. Students are isolated from family, friends, and familiar surroundings. Most could not walk home if needed. Some are from overseas. Limited funds characterize these students, so many will be unable to budget for survival equipment, travel home, or perhaps even for the purchase of basic food supplies.

Who is responsible in the event of a major problem? The people will need directions and a means of maintaining order, particularly if they cannot discover the effects of Y2K the world over. Someone will rise up and take control. If there is no strong leadership, confusion and panic will come into play. Students will need food, warmth, and, above all, a connection to their families.

As a parent, you'll want to know where your child is and what the institution has planned in case of emergency. We encourage you to find out if there is an emergency plan already in existence. If so, get a copy, examine it closely, and know what the university expects you to do. Know who is supposed to be in charge and what their duties are, then communicate that information to your son or daughter. You should know where to meet, what equipment to use, and who will be making the decisions on campus.

Talk to your child about some basic questions: How would you get home? Would you need to check out with someone, or can you leave on your own? How would you let us know you are OK? If a long-term disruption occurs because of Y2K, would you want to continue your studies for the semester, or drop it and wait awhile? If so, who would you report to and what would be the requirements? How would you be tested? Could your money be refunded?

The hard truth is that without planning, your son or daughter could be in the midst of a disaster. Take time now to talk with your college-age child about Y2K survival plans.

The Two- to Three-Day Plan

If you live in an apartment and believe Y2K will last only a few days, there are five things you should do. First, work out a plan with your neighbors. Write it down so you are clear as to what you will do. Second, invest in some emergency food and supplies, like a camp stove, flashlight, and battery-powered radio. You don't have to spend a fortune, but you should at least be ready to last a few days on your own.

Third, contact your friends and relatives before January 1, so that they know your plan. If things were to get worse, you can always leave your apartment and join them. Fourth, band together with your neighbors to protect yourself and others around you. The more discussion you have with them, the better prepared you'll be. Fifth, be willing to be flexible. If things start to go bad, have a backup plan in place.

The One-Month Plan

Planning to survive a month of troubles in your apartment will take some doing. You're going to need to have other people you can count on to help you, who will help you get ready and perhaps help invest in the things you need. Of utmost importance is adequate food and water, along with a convenient place to store it. *Make this your first priority*, and talk with your neighbors about security and safety issues.

Heating may prove to be the biggest problem in northern climates, so reflect on what you'll do if you have no electricity or gas. A portable propane heater may work for a while, but a fireplace or wood stove would be better. Warm clothes, a heavy sleeping bag, and plenty of blankets are necessities.

You should also have some money or gold hidden in your apartment, along with a radio, books, and adequate lighting. You're going to need a plan for getting rid of garbage, so think about investing in a shovel and a chemical toilet, then look for a place to bury solid waste. And by all means consider how you will contact family and friends in other cities—investing in a cell phone might be a good idea. Finally, think through your transportation options. If you need to leave your apartment for whatever reason, you'll want some reliable transportation at the ready. Talk to someone about visiting, fill your car with gas, and map out the best route to get there safely.

The One-Year Plan

If you believe the effects of Y2K could last one year, you probably are not planning to spend it in an apartment. Establish a network of people you can trust and depend on, and talk with them about your long-term plans. You will need a significant supply of food—probably more than you can store in an apartment—and a source of adequate drinking water. You'll also need to consider staying warm and dry, stocking up on medical supplies, and finding a way to keep up on the outside world.

You will no doubt want to seek some alternative long-term living arrangement. Perhaps you could join a family in the country, or seek work on a farm or ranch. Invest in gold coins if at all possible, and have them ready to use when you need them.

No one wants to go through disasters, but they are bound to occur in our lives. Our survival in an emergency like Y2K usually depends on our preparation, our attitude, and our ability to work with others. Set up a plan you believe in and keep your faith in God. You can do it. You can survive.

YOUR Y2K PLANNING GUIDE

Ten Questions to Ask About Apartment Living

1. Do you feel safe in your apartment?
2. Could the police or fire department find you quickly and easily in an emergency?
3. Do you know your neighbors? Do you trust them?
4. Who lives close to you that would require help during a Y2K emergency?
5. Would anyone in your building join you in purchasing bulk foods? Would they join you in buying essential supplies?
6. How would you heat your apartment?
7. How would you take care of solid waste?
8. What activities would you do to fill your hours?
9. Have you an emergency kit in your car? Do you carry one in a backpack?
10. If staying at your apartment didn't work out, where could you go?

TWENTY

Part of the Community

Perhaps the greatest test of our social system in the United States will come when our neighborliness is put on the line. If you have adequately prepared but your neighbor has not, will you share? Will you help? Part of the "American way" is to expect people to stand on their own two feet, and if someone else has a problem, we think it's the person's own fault. *The best strategy when preparing for Y2K is to extend your efforts on a community-wide basis.* Unless your approach is to get as far away from other people as possible to become completely self-sufficient, a community of prepared families is probably the best place to be. A community of unprepared families may be the worst place to be, regardless of how much compassion and concern you have for one another. Compassion doesn't stretch very far without resources.

Y2K might be the catalyst for the most revolutionary tearing down of walls between neighbors since the Berlin Wall was breached. This might be the time when you finally meet your nearby neighbors as you collaborate on community

What's Ahead

- **Start at Home and Work Outward**

- **What if Y2K Is a Lamb instead of a Lion?**

- **Ready or Not, Here Comes Y2K**

- **Panic, Paralysis, or Preparation?**

preparedness. Even if the worst-case scenarios play out in their most gruesome fashion, those who are united in community around the common purpose of responding to the disaster will fare better than those who try to go it alone.

Because levels of readiness will vary from house to house and street to street, most advisers recommend that families not flaunt their preparedness. That's one reason why you should establish your neighborhood or community interdependence before the need arises. Once the crisis hits, fear and uncertainty may combine to elevate self-preservation to a higher value than community well-being and compassionate sharing. Crises bring out the best and the worst in people. Find out now whom you can trust and develop a plan for working together.

If the impact of Y2K is as widespread as it potentially could be, local relief will have to come from local sources. If communications and transportation systems are adversely affected, disaster relief from outside your local area may not be possible. Local community preparedness will be the best option.

Start at Home and Work Outward

In the same way that a simple two-digit date code in a single computer can reach out and affect an entire network, the answer to Y2K preparedness begins with individual families preparing their own disaster-relief plan, then brancning out to develop neighborhood and community plans, which in turn can be linked with other communities to compose regional plans. *The most important step for you to take is the first one, which is to begin to prepare a personal readiness plan.*

You need a strategy that will work where you live. If you have a yard where you can plant vegetables, for example, you will have an advantage over the apartment dweller who only has a window box, but both of you can take steps to prepare. Our objective is to help you be as well-prepared as you can be, given the realities of your present circumstances and the limits of your present resources. So prepare yourself, encourage your friends and neighbors to prepare themselves, and increasingly widen your circle of preparedness.

What if Y2K Is a Lamb Instead of a Lion?

What happens if you plan for catastrophe, and reality is a bump in the road? *Think of your contingency plan as an insurance policy.* If you're like most people, you already pay premiums for protection in the event of circumstances you never want to face. When your house burns down, your son breaks his arm, or you wrap your car around a tree, you're happy to have the insurance. Even the optimists are conceding at least some disruption will be caused by Y2K, so having some sort of "insurance" seems prudent. It may not be a head-on collision, but a fender bender is almost guaranteed.

If you pay into an auto insurance policy for ten years and never have an accident, your premium dollars are gone and you gain no residual benefit. But in the case of Y2K, most of the preparations you make will be consistent with your everyday needs even if the worst-case scenarios never materialize. Cash reserves can be redeposited or reinvested, food reserves will still be edible (and you won't have to shop as often for a while!), wood stoves and firewood will still heat your home, and may well prove to be more efficient than your current system. In the process of prioritizing your needs, you may make some surprising discoveries about what you can do without. And by all means, speak to experts in your area before making significant decisions.

Even if you overprepare for Y2K, your readiness may come in handy when an unforeseen weather system knocks out power in your area. So if Y2K turns out to be a minor disaster rather than a major debacle, you and your community will be prepared for other disasters. If no disaster of any size strikes, you'll have on hand a stockpile of resources you can gradually consume over the next few months.

Ready or Not, Here Comes Y2K

Nobody likes to look at worst-case scenarios, but unless you at least consider the possibility that every dire warning you've heard could come true, you will not be adequately prepared. When the new year dawns, not having electricity might soon be the least of your worries. Even on the bleakest of days, the sun will still rise. No matter how long or short the crisis is, food, water, clothing, and shelter will always be your top priorities. If you live in a severe climate (hot or cold), you can add heating or cooling as a necessary component of any shelter you have.

If Y2K hits with full force, transportation and telecommunications are likely to be snarled, the banks will probably be closed, and a declaration of martial law is not out of the question. Reliable information might be hard to come by, so it may be awhile before any of these shutdowns are confirmed. The good news (if there is any) in a protracted bank shutdown is that no one will be in a hurry to foreclose on your house, so even if you are not able to make your payments, you will most likely have a place to live. Also, if electronic transfers are curtailed, you won't be able to pay your other bills, which will free up the cash you have set aside to procure any of the bare necessities of life that you were unable to set aside beforehand. Of course, if the banking system collapses, the repercussions will be catastrophic, but then we are discussing a worst-case scenario here—and the banks are vulnerable.

If you have stockpiled an adequate supply of food and water, your first few days may be spent sitting around the fire telling stories from your childhood or playing nonelectronic games. You may be surprised to find how easy it is to quit watching television. By day four or five, the novelty will have long worn off and you will be carefully reviewing your contingency plans and rationing your supplies.

If the crisis extends into a second week, personal security and protecting your assets will become an increasing priority. Here is where community preparedness will become vital. Any opportunistic marauders will pick on the weak and isolated before they will contend with a well-organized neighborhood group. You will have to decide in advance how far you are willing to go to defend yourselves and how far you are willing to go in sharing your supplies with others who have not adequately prepared. Will you incorporate the weak and isolated into your community? By working together as a neighborhood or community, you will gain the strength of numbers and the benefit of a wider pool of gifts, abilities, and resources.

When spring arrives, if the disruptions in society continue that long, the group will want to turn its attention to longer-range food supplies. If you have planned well and included a supply of nonhybrid seeds, you will be prepared to cultivate food to carry you through the months to come. Of course, you'll have to grow it first and then protect it from those who would glean your fields without your permission, but by this time you will be more accustomed to hard work, and any denial you have been harboring should just about be gone. Here again, community preparedness will make these otherwise daunting tasks more feasible. The longer the Y2K problems last, the more important preparation and community cooperation will be.

Panic, Paralysis, or Preparation?

Everyone who is busily putting together a survival plan today has had to come to grips with the mind-boggling possibilities that accompany Y2K. Most of us who have grown up in the post-World War II era have a hard time imagining that everything we've accumulated and built could collapse. Nobody wants to believe it, but the evidence is startling. The first question you must answer is, "How seriously are you going to take all of this?" Can you afford to be wrong on the side of underpreparation? Can you take reasonable steps to at least cut your risk if not totally prepare for hard times? This book is written for those who are willing to look the possibility of danger in the eye and develop a solid plan.

Don't panic, but also don't delay. Take Y2K seriously. If you haven't looked closely at the facts, wake up and get busy.

Evaluate the available information and use the chapters in this book to help you develop a plan for emergency readiness. If you wait until you hear the shout in the courtyard before you start to prepare, you will likely discover that all of the "lamp oil" is either gone or prohibitively expensive. The longer you delay, the worse your chances for success and the more drastic your options will be.

RECOMMENDED RESOURCES

American Survival Guide, a magazine from American Survival
The Complete Survival Guide, by Mark Thiffault, ed. (DBI Books, 1988)
The Day the World Shuts Down, by Levy and Hafner (Regnery Publishing, 1998)
How to Develop a Low-Cost Family Food Storage System,
    by Anita Evangelista (Breakout Productions, 1995)
How to Do Just About Anything, by the Reader's Digest Staff
    (Reader's Digest Books, 1997)
Live Off the Land in the City and Country, by Ragnar Benson
    (Delta Press, 1987)
The Millennium Bug, by Michael S. Hyatt (Regnery Publishing, 1998)
The Natural Foods Epicure, by Nancy Albright (Hampton Roads Publishing
    Company, 1992)
The Survivalists Medicine Chest, by Ragnar Benson (Paladin Press, 1978)
Time Bomb 2000, by Ed and Jennifer Yourdon (Prentice Hall, 1997)
Wright's Complete Disaster Survival Manual, by Ted Wright (Hampton Roads
    Publishing Company, 1993)

Web Sites You May Want to Explore

Gary North's Y2K Links (www.garynorth.com)
Michael Hyatt's Y2K Website (www.michaelhyatt.com)
The Joseph Project (www.josephproject2000.org)
The Millennia Project (www.millennia-bcs.com)
The Mother of All Y2K Link Centers (http://pw2.netcom.com)
United StatesY2K and You (www.itpolicy.gsa.gov/mks/yr2000/y2khome.htm)
Westergaard Year 2000 (www.y2ktimebomb.com)
Y2K News (www.y2knews.com)
Y2K Today (www.y2ktoday.com)
Y2K Watch (www.y2kwatch.com)
Year 2000 Information Center (www.year2000.com)

ABOUT THE AUTHORS

Jerry MacGregor, Ph.D., is a senior editor at Harvest House Publishers. Jerry has helped create more than 80 books, writing on such diverse topics as sleight-of-hand magic, parenting, and the lure of cults. Some of his short stories can be seen in the #1 bestseller *Stories for the Heart.* Jerry holds a master's degree from Biola University and a doctorate in organizational development from the University of Oregon. He often presents his *Mind Games* lecture to groups, exposing psychic frauds and the false spiritual phenomena in our culture. He and his family live in Eugene, Oregon.

Kirk Charles is a writer with more than 40 titles to his credit. A graduate of Kansas State University, he teaches memory workshops around the country, and is available to speak to groups about the effects of Y2K on the culture. He and his wife live in Seattle, Washington, with their two cats, Grim and Asta.

The authors wish to acknowledge . . .

Dave Lindstedt, a free-lance writer and editor with a background in printing and advertising, who helped create the first section of this book. During the past five years, Dave has created a portable career while researching the issues of self-sufficient living and small-scale sustainable agriculture. A graduate of the University of Oregon School of Journalism, he lives with his wife and four children in Oregon. The seven effects detailed in chapter 2 are Dave's thoughts, and we thank him for his wisdom and writing skill.

Duane Young, a free-lance writer from Oregon, who helped with the creation of Part 4. A longtime pastor and teacher, Duane lives with his wife and their five children in Portland. His research and writing helped us get this book done on time, and we appreciate his hard work.

If you would like someone to speak to your group about Y2K and the best way to prepare for it, please contact the authors through Harvest House Publishers, 1075 Arrowsmith, Eugene, OR 97402.

NOTES

NOTES

NOTES

NOTES

_____

_____

_____

_____

_____

_____

_____

_____

_____

_____

_____

_____

_____

_____

_____

_____

_____

_____

_____

_____

_____

_____

_____

_____

_____

_____

NOTES

NOTES

Other Good
Harvest House Reading

MIND GAMES
by *André Kole* and *Jerry MacGregor*

Psychic readings, identifying unseen objects, psychic surgery—miracles or illusions? Drawing from his experience and study, Kole provides clear explanations for supposed miracles and wonders and reveals the trickery behind astrology, UFOs, ghosts, and more.

FAMILY TIMES
by *Jerry* and *Patti MacGregor*

Family Times is the perfect resource for creative, let's-have-fun opportunities that build open communication, acceptance, teamwork, and Christian values at home.

MORE FOR YOUR MONEY
by *James Paris*

This newly revised and expanded combination of the popular *Living Financially Free* and *Living Financially Free Workbook* is bursting with everything you need to manage your money in a God-honoring way. Christian consumer advocate Jim Paris shows you how to set up a budget, understand the new tax laws, and more.

**Y2K: A REASONED RESPONSE
TO MASS HYSTERIA**
by *Dave Hunt*

Dave Hunt's careful investigation, including interviews with top management and computer experts, reveals a problem of manageable proportions and provides reasonable answers to the questions that people are asking about the effects of the Y2K computer problem.

Dear Reader,

We would appreciate hearing from you regarding this Harvest House nonfiction book. It will enable us to continue to give you the best in Christian publishing.

1. What most influenced you to purchase *The Y2K Family Survival Guide?*
   - ❑ Author
   - ❑ Subject matter
   - ❑ Backcover copy
   - ❑ Recommendations
   - ❑ Cover/Title
   - ❑ Other_____

2. Where did you purchase this book?
   - ❑ Christian bookstore
   - ❑ General bookstore
   - ❑ Department store
   - ❑ Grocery store
   - ❑ Other_____

3. Your overall rating of this book?
   ❑ Excellent   ❑ Very good   ❑ Good   ❑ Fair   ❑ Poor

4. How likely would you be to purchase other books by this author?
   ❑ Very likely   ❑ Not very likely   ❑ Somewhat likely   ❑ Not at all

5. What types of books most interest you? (Check all that apply.)
   - ❑ Women's Books
   - ❑ Marriage Books
   - ❑ Current Issues
   - ❑ Christian Living
   - ❑ Bible Studies
   - ❑ Fiction
   - ❑ Biographies
   - ❑ Children's Books
   - ❑ Youth Books
   - ❑ Other_____

6. Please check the box next to your age group.
   ❑ Under 18   ❑ 18-24   ❑ 25-34   ❑ 35-44   ❑ 45-54   ❑ 55 and over

Mail to: Editorial Director
Harvest House Publishers
1075 Arrowsmith
Eugene, OR 97402

Name_____

Address _____

State _____ Zip _____

Thank you for helping us to help you in future publications!